THE POWER OF DAILY QUESTIONS

TRANSFORMING YOUR WORLD "ONE QUESTION AT A TIME"

Columbus Njikem

Copyright © 2023 by Columbus Njikem

All rights reserved.

The content contained within this book may not be reproduced, duplicated or transmitted without direct written permission from the author or the publisher.

Contents

Introduction: 5

Chapter 1: Setting the Stage 7

PART I: THE IMPORTANCE OF SELF-REFLECTION 28

Chapter 2: The Art of Self-Inquiry 29

Chapter 3: Daily Question Rituals 34

PART II: 40

EMBRACING PROACTIVITY AND PROBLEM-SOLVING 40

Chapter 4: Be the Change You Seek 41

Chapter 5: Opportunities in Problem-Solving 51

Part III: Cultivating an Opportunity Mindset 57

Chapter 6: Unleashing Your Potential: The Power of Personal Daily Questions 58

Chapter 7: Creating Positive Change 65

PART IV: INSPIRING ACTION AND TRANSFORMATION 70

Chapter 8: From Craving to Contentment 71

Chapter 9: The Ripple Effect of Change 81

Chapter 10: Your Journey Begins - Key Takeaways from "The Power of Daily Questions: Transforming Your World One Question at a Time" 86

Appendices 91

Acknowledgments: 97

Author's Note: 98

Introduction:

Welcome to "The Power of Daily Questions: Transforming Your World One Question at a Time." In the bustling tapestry of our lives, we often find ourselves seeking answers to questions that shape our destinies. Yet, in our quest for change, growth, and understanding, we tend to underestimate the transformative potential of the questions themselves.

This book is a journey, an exploration of how asking the right questions to yourself each day can become a guiding force in your life, leading you towards a path of self-discovery, personal growth, and the creation of a more purposeful and fulfilling existence.

Here, we delve into the profound idea that questions host answers in the world we inhabit. The power of daily questions is not just a theoretical concept; it's a practical tool that can ignite your curiosity, unlock your potential, and initiate a positive ripple effect in your life and the lives of those around you.

Throughout the chapters of this book, we'll embark on a voyage that touches upon various aspects of personal development, problem-solving, mindfulness, leadership, gratitude, and the art of creating positive change in your environment. You'll discover that the answers to life's most intricate questions often reside within your own ability to ask, reflect, and take action.

Prepare to journey through real-life stories of individuals who harnessed the transformative energy of daily questions to transcend obstacles, discover their latent potential, and inspire change on a grand scale. As you read, you'll find practical exercises, journaling templates, and recommended readings to guide you on your personal quest for growth and self-improvement.

This book is more than just words on pages; it's an invitation to a daily practice that has the potential to shape the trajectory of your life. It's a call to action, a journey of self-discovery, and a guide to transforming your world, one question at a time.

Are you ready to embrace the transformative power of daily questions? The adventure begins now.

Chapter 1:

Setting the Stage

In the opening chapter, 'Setting the Stage,' we lay the foundation for a profound exploration of personal transformation and growth. It is within this chapter that we establish the fundamental principles and perspectives that will guide our journey. Here, we delve into the significance of self-awareness, the power of intention, and the importance of a growth mindset. As we embark on this transformative journey together, 'Setting the Stage' serves as a compass, helping us navigate the complexities of personal development, empowerment, and the pursuit of a more fulfilling and successful life.

In a world where change is the only constant, we often find ourselves waiting for external circumstances to shift in our favor. We wait for that promotion, that stroke of luck, or that magical moment when our dreams will finally come true. But what if I told you that the key to unlocking the life you desire isn't found in the waiting game? What if I revealed that the path to success, fulfillment, and prosperity begins with you, right now?

Welcome to "The Power of Daily Questions: Transforming Your World One Question at a Time." In the pages that follow, we'll embark on a journey of self-discovery and proactive change. It's a journey that will challenge your perspectives, ignite your ambition, and unveil the incredible potential that resides within you.

Proactive Change: The Success-Oriented Mindset

Success isn't a destination; it's a mindset. It's the understanding that waiting for things to change for you is a passive approach, while actively shaping your reality is the true path to success. This book is about embracing a success-oriented mindset that empowers you to take control of your life and create the opportunities you seek.

Consider this scenario: a diverse group of individuals, each hailing from different backgrounds and cultures, coming together to work on a common goal. At first glance, it may seem like a recipe for conflict and chaos. Differences in interpretation, methods, and priorities can easily lead to misunderstandings and even clashes of interest. But herein lies the essence of proactive change.

Embracing Diversity as an Opportunity

When things don't align with our preferences and expectations, when we face challenges and conflicts, these moments become the fertile soil in which opportunities flourish. It's in these very situations that the proactive individual stands out by adapting, problem-solving, and forging meaningful connections.

Consider asking questions like, "What can I do to help my colleague from a different background feel included?" or "How can I adapt my approach to work collaboratively with others who see things differently?" These questions are the keys to unlocking your ability to create positive change in your environment.

Taking Control of Your Journey

"The Power of Daily Questions" is not just a book; it's a roadmap to a more fulfilling and successful life. It's an invitation to take control of your journey, to ask the right questions, and to proactively shape the world around you. In the chapters that follow, we will delve into the art of self-inquiry, the significance of daily question rituals, and the transformative impact of a success-oriented mindset.

Are you ready to begin your journey of proactive change? It starts with the very first question. Let's explore the power of daily questions and learn how, by transforming our thinking and actions one question at a time, we can unlock a world of opportunities, success, and prosperity.

Join me as we embark on this transformative journey together.

Self-reflection and awareness play a fundamental role in succeeding with daily questions for personal growth. These aspects are the cornerstone of using daily questions effectively, as they enable individuals to gain deeper insights into themselves and their lives. Here's why self-reflection and awareness are crucial:

Identifying Strengths and Weaknesses: Self-reflection allows you to recognize your strengths and weaknesses with clarity. By asking questions like, "What am I good at?" and "What areas do I need to improve in?" you gain a better understanding of your abilities. This knowledge empowers you to build on your strengths and address your weaknesses strategically.

Setting Meaningful Goals: Awareness of your values, desires, and passions is essential for setting meaningful goals. When you reflect on what truly matters to you, you can craft goals that align with your authentic self. Daily questions such as, "What are my long-term aspirations?" help you define your life's purpose and direction.

Tracking Progress: Self-awareness enables you to monitor your progress effectively. By regularly assessing your actions and outcomes, you can determine if you are moving closer to your goals or need to make adjustments. Questions like, "Am I taking steps toward my goals?" keep you accountable for your actions.

Emotional Intelligence: Self-reflection fosters emotional intelligence, which is crucial for personal growth. By asking questions like, "How am I feeling today?" or "Why did I react that way?" you can explore your emotions, understand their triggers, and develop better emotional regulation skills.

Improved Decision-Making: Self-awareness enhances decision-making. When you are in tune with your values and priorities, you can make choices that align with your long-term objectives. Daily questions like, "Does this decision align with my values?" help ensure your choices are in harmony with your personal growth journey.

Building Resilience: Self-reflection allows you to learn from setbacks and failures. By asking questions such as, "What did I learn from this experience?" You can turn challenges into valuable lessons. This resilience is essential for overcoming obstacles on your path to personal growth.

Enhanced Relationships: Self-awareness extends to how you relate to others. By reflecting on your communication style, empathy, and interpersonal dynamics, you can improve your relationships. Daily questions like, "How can I be a better listener?" or "How can I show more empathy today?" can lead to stronger connections with others.

Adaptability: Self-awareness helps you adapt to change more effectively. By understanding your strengths and areas for development, you can adjust your approach as circumstances evolve. Questions like, "How can I adapt to this new situation?" foster adaptability and resilience.

Increased Accountability: Self-reflection holds you accountable for your actions and choices. When you regularly ask questions like, "Am I living in alignment with my values?" or "What can I do differently to achieve my goals?" You take ownership of your life and actively work toward your personal growth.

In the labyrinth of life's uncertainties and endless possibilities, the beacon that guides us toward our dreams and aspirations is clarity of goals. It is the roadmap that transforms vague desires into well-defined objectives, and it is the catalyst for meaningful personal growth. Clarity of goals is the North Star that keeps us on course, and daily questioning is the compass that ensures we stay true to our path.

Defining the Destination

Imagine standing at the crossroads of life, facing countless directions to choose from. Without clear goals, these paths seem equally enticing and perplexing. This is where daily questioning steps in as the clarifying force. When we ask ourselves, "What do I truly want to achieve?" or "What is my ultimate dream?" we begin to carve out our destination in the vast landscape of possibilities.

Clarity of goals means going beyond the surface-level wishes and digging deeper into our aspirations. It's about deciphering the difference between vague ambitions like "I want to be successful" and well-defined goals such as "I want to start my own business and achieve financial independence within the next five years." The former is a nebulous notion, while the latter is a concrete objective that can be broken down into actionable steps.

Breaking Down the Journey

Daily questions provide the structure needed to break down the journey toward our goals into manageable milestones. They prompt us to ask, "What steps can I take today to get closer to my goal?" or "What skills and knowledge do I need to acquire to reach my destination?" These questions transform the abstract into the actionable.

For instance, if your dream goal is to become a published author, daily questions might include, "What can I write today to progress my book?" or "How can I improve my writing skills?" Each question guides you toward tangible actions that accumulate over time, bringing your goal within reach.

Measuring Progress

Clarity of goals isn't static; it evolves as you progress. Daily questions help you stay connected with your aspirations and monitor your journey's trajectory. Questions like, "Am I on track to achieve my goals?" or "Have my priorities shifted, and do I need to adjust my objectives?" allow you to recalibrate and realign as needed.

Furthermore, daily questioning enables you to celebrate your achievements, both big and small. By regularly asking, "What have I accomplished today that aligns with my goals?" You acknowledge your progress and stay motivated to keep moving forward.

Life is rife with challenges and obstacles, and how we navigate them often determines our path to success. Problem-solving is not just a skill; it's a mindset, and it's one that thrives on the power of questions. When confronted with dilemmas, setbacks, or seemingly insurmountable barriers, questions become the key to unlocking our problem-solving abilities and discovering innovative solutions.

The Role of Questions in Problem Solving

Problems are like puzzles, waiting to be deciphered, and questions are the tools we use to solve them. Questions prompt us to examine the challenge from different angles, break it down into manageable parts, and explore potential approaches. They open the door to critical thinking, creativity, and ingenuity.

When faced with a problem, the natural response is to ask, "How can I overcome this?" or "What can I do to fix it?" These initial questions set the problem-solving process in motion. They stimulate our cognitive faculties, such as analysis, synthesis, and evaluation, and encourage us to explore potential solutions.

Stimulating Creativity

Beyond the standard questions, creative problem-solving often requires asking unconventional or open-ended questions. For example:

- "What if I approached this problem from a completely different perspective?"
- "Are there any analogies or metaphors that can help me understand this challenge better?"
- "How might someone from a completely different field or background approach this problem?"

These questions break us free from conventional thinking patterns and open the door to novel ideas and innovative solutions. They encourage us to step outside our comfort zones and explore uncharted territories, where creativity thrives.

Iterative Problem-Solving

The process of problem-solving is rarely linear. It often involves cycles of questioning, experimentation, evaluation, and adaptation. Each cycle refines our understanding of the problem and brings us closer to a viable solution.

Questions play a pivotal role in this iterative process. We ask, "What have I learned from my previous attempts?" or "How can I adjust my approach based on these insights?" These questions enable us to fine-tune our strategies and navigate the ever-evolving landscape of a complex problem.

Collaborative Problem-Solving

Questions aren't limited to our internal dialogue. They are also powerful tools for collaborative problem-solving. When faced with a challenge as a team, asking questions like, "What are your thoughts on this issue?" or "How do you perceive the problem?" encourages diverse perspectives and collective brainstorming. It fosters an environment where everyone's input is valued, and innovative solutions can emerge.

The Satisfaction of Resolution

Ultimately, problem-solving is not just about finding solutions; it's about the satisfaction that comes from overcoming obstacles. When we pose questions and actively engage in the problem-solving process, we gain a sense of agency and control over our circumstances.

Moreover, the act of solving problems and overcoming challenges strengthens our problem-solving abilities for future endeavors. It's a skill that compounds over time, empowering us to tackle increasingly complex issues with confidence and resilience.

Empowering Decision-Making

Clear goals become the cornerstone of informed decision-making. When faced with choices, whether personal or professional, you can evaluate them against your goals. Questions like, "Does this decision align with my long-term objectives?" or "Will this choice bring me closer to my dream goal?" empower you to make choices that resonate with your aspirations.

Problem Solving

Life is replete with challenges and hurdles, both big and small, and often, the seeds of problem-solving are sown in the very soil of our immediate environment. Whether it's a minor inconvenience at home or a complex issue at work, questions are the stepping stones that guide us through the maze of difficulties. Problem-solving, as a skill, begins with the act of asking questions and navigating the path to creative solutions.

The Proximity of Problems

Our immediate environment is where we encounter problems most frequently. It's where we face everyday dilemmas and disruptions that require swift resolution. These issues could range from a malfunctioning household appliance to a disagreement with a coworker. These challenges may appear mundane, but they are the building blocks of our problem-solving prowess.

When confronted with an issue in your immediate environment, questions naturally arise. "How can I fix this?" or "What steps can I take to address this problem?" become the impetus for action. By asking these initial questions, you engage your problem-solving abilities and set the wheels of solution-seeking in motion.

Stimulating Creativity and Innovation

The act of asking questions isn't limited to seeking standard answers; it's also a gateway to creativity and innovation. Beyond the customary queries, you might wonder, "Is there a more efficient way to do this?" or "What can I learn from this situation?" These open-ended questions encourage you to explore unconventional approaches and perspectives.

For instance, when faced with a malfunctioning household appliance, you might ask, "Can I repurpose this item in a creative way?" or "What design flaws led to this issue, and how could they be improved?" These questions can lead to innovative solutions and even spark your creativity.

The Iterative Nature of Problem-Solving

Problem-solving is rarely a one-and-done affair. It's an iterative process that involves cycles of questioning, experimenting, evaluating, and adapting. With each iteration, your understanding of the problem deepens, and you move closer to a viable solution.

Questions play a pivotal role in this iterative process. You might ask, "What did I learn from my previous attempts?" or "How can I refine my approach based on these insights?" These questions guide your problem-solving journey, helping you adjust your strategies and navigate the evolving landscape of the challenge.

The Personal and Collective Impact

While problem-solving often begins with questions directed toward one's immediate environment, it can have a profound impact on both personal growth and collective progress. The act of seeking solutions cultivates resilience, adaptability, and critical thinking skills. It empowers individuals to confront larger and more complex issues in various aspects of life.

Moreover, in a collaborative context, questions become bridges to effective teamwork and collective problem-solving. When people come together to address a common challenge, asking questions like, "What are your thoughts on this issue?" or "How can we approach this problem as a team?" fosters collaboration, diversity of thought, and innovative solutions.

The essence of human progress is rooted in our innate curiosity and the insatiable thirst for knowledge. At the heart of this pursuit lies the power of questions. Questions are not just tools for seeking answers; they are the catalysts that fuel our quest for continuous learning and growth. They are the key to unlocking the vast expanse of human understanding and expanding our horizons.

The Inherent Curiosity

From the moment we are born, curiosity is woven into the very fabric of our being. It's what drives us to explore our surroundings, to touch, taste, and discover the world. As we grow, this curiosity evolves into a more refined form—intellectual curiosity. We begin to ask questions not just about the physical world but also about abstract concepts, ideas, and the mysteries of life.

Questions are the manifestation of this curiosity. They are the verbal or mental expression of our desire to understand, to make sense of the unknown, and to grasp the intricacies of our existence.

The Pursuit of Knowledge

Questions serve as the compass that directs our pursuit of knowledge. When you ask, "How does this work?" or "Why does this happen?" you embark on a journey of discovery. This pursuit can take many forms: from reading books and conducting experiments to engaging in conversations and seeking mentors.

In the digital age, the power of questions is amplified. We have access to vast repositories of information at our fingertips, and questions serve as the gateway to this treasure trove of knowledge. By asking the right questions, you navigate this sea of information and extract meaningful insights.

The Expansion of Horizons

Questions have the remarkable ability to expand our horizons. They prompt us to explore unfamiliar subjects and venture into uncharted territories. A question like, "What can I learn from a different culture?" can lead to the exploration of history, traditions, and perspectives that broaden our understanding of the world.

Moreover, questions foster a growth mindset. When you ask, "How can I improve in this area?" or "What skills can I acquire?" you embrace the belief that your abilities can be developed through dedication and hard work. This mindset propels you to take on new challenges and strive for personal growth.

Embracing the Unknown

Questions are not just about finding answers; they are about embracing the unknown. They remind us that there is always more to learn, discover, and explore. In a rapidly changing world, the ability to ask questions is a survival skill. It's the means by which we adapt, innovate, and stay relevant.

Questions are also an integral part of critical thinking. They encourage us to evaluate information, consider different perspectives, and make informed decisions. By asking questions like, "What evidence supports this claim?" or "What are the potential consequences of this decision?" we become more discerning and responsible individuals.

A Lifelong Journey

Finally, learning and growth are lifelong journeys, and questions are our faithful companions on this odyssey. They ignite our curiosity, guide us in our pursuit of knowledge, and expand the horizons of our understanding. Through questions, we not only seek answers but also embrace the beauty of the unknown. They are the sparks that kindle the flames of learning and growth throughout our lives.

Positive Mindset: Illuminating Life's Brighter Aspects Through Questions

In the tapestry of existence, the threads of positivity and optimism weave a vibrant pattern that colors our experiences. The art of cultivating a positive mindset often begins with the questions we ask ourselves daily. Questions are not just inquiries; they are instruments that can frame our thoughts and perspectives, guiding us toward the sunny side of life. When we pose questions that promote positivity, we embark on a transformative journey of gratitude, kindness, and a heightened awareness of life's brighter aspects.

The Power of Framing

Our thoughts are shaped by the questions we entertain. When we ask, "What can I be grateful for today?" or "How can I make a positive impact on someone's life?" we are consciously choosing to frame our mindset in a positive light. These questions act as a lens that focuses our attention on the positive elements of our daily existence.

Cultivating Gratitude

One of the most potent ways to foster a positive mindset is by cultivating gratitude. Daily questions that center around gratitude, such as "What am I thankful for today?" or "Who has brought joy into my life recently?" encourage us to reflect on the abundance that surrounds us. They remind us that even in the midst of challenges, there are countless blessings to appreciate.

Gratitude not only shifts our focus from what we lack to what we have but also has a profound impact on our well-being. Research has shown that practicing gratitude can enhance our mood, reduce stress, and improve overall life satisfaction. Daily gratitude questions, when incorporated into our routine, become a transformative force that elevates our emotional and mental state.

Spreading Positivity Through Actions

Positivity is not just an internal state of mind; it is a force that radiates outward, touching the lives of those around us. Daily questions that encourage us to ask, "How can I make a positive impact on someone's life?" or "What act of kindness can I perform today?" empower us to be agents of positive change in our communities.

When we actively seek opportunities to bring joy, support, or encouragement to others, we not only brighten their day but also enhance our own sense of purpose and fulfillment. Acts of kindness, prompted by positive questions, create a ripple effect of positivity that extends far beyond our immediate interactions.

Embracing Life's Brighter Aspects

A positive mindset is not the denial of life's challenges but rather the choice to focus on the brighter aspects of life despite those challenges. Daily questions that promote positivity serve as our compass, guiding us toward these brighter aspects. They remind us that even on the stormiest days, there is a ray of sunshine to be found.

Adaptability: Thriving in a Dynamic World Through Questions

In today's fast-paced and ever-changing world, adaptability has become a cornerstone of personal and professional success. The ability to pivot, evolve, and thrive in the face of new situations and challenges is a crucial skill. To cultivate this skill, one must harness the power of questions. Questions act as the compass that guides us through the uncharted waters of change, keeping us flexible, open-minded, and ready to embrace whatever the world throws our way.

The Accelerating Pace of Change

The world we live in is characterized by rapid and relentless change. Technological advancements, global shifts, and unforeseen events can alter the landscape of our personal and professional lives in the blink of an eye. In this environment, adaptability is no longer a nice-to-have; it's a necessity.

Questions as the Catalyst for Adaptation

Adaptability begins with questions. When we ask, "How can I adapt to this new situation?" or "What changes can I make to thrive in this evolving landscape?" we signal our readiness to face change head-on. These questions prompt us to explore new strategies, perspectives, and approaches.

Flexibility Through Self-Examination

Adaptability often starts with self-examination. Questions like, "What are my strengths and weaknesses in this context?" or "What skills do I need to develop to navigate this change effectively?" encourage us to assess our readiness for the challenges ahead. By identifying areas where we can improve, we position ourselves to adapt more seamlessly.

Openness to New Ideas

Adaptability is also closely tied to openness to new ideas and perspectives. Questions such as, "What can I learn from others who have successfully adapted to similar changes?" or "How can I incorporate innovative solutions into my approach?" push us beyond our comfort zones. They encourage us to seek guidance, collaborate, and embrace fresh ideas.

Remaining Agile in Decision-Making

In a rapidly changing world, decision-making is a dynamic process. Questions like, "What new information has emerged that might impact my decisions?" or "How can I adjust my strategy based on the latest developments?" remind us that adaptability is an ongoing journey. It's about staying agile and responsive to the evolving circumstances around us.

Resilience Through Problem-Solving

Adaptability is not just about reacting to change but also about proactively solving problems that arise from it. Questions such as, "What challenges might I encounter in this new environment?" or "How can I anticipate and address potential obstacles?" equip us with the tools to navigate change with resilience.

Embracing the Unknown

Ultimately, adaptability is about embracing the unknown with a sense of curiosity and confidence. Questions are the bridge to this mindset. They encourage us to ask, "What opportunities might this change bring?" or "How can I use this challenge as a steppingstone to personal and professional growth?" These questions empower us to transform uncertainty into opportunity.

The Lifelong Skill of Adaptability

In a world where change is the only constant, adaptability is not just a skill; it's a lifelong journey. Questions are the fuel that propels us on this journey. They remind us that adaptability is not a destination but a way of life. By consistently asking the right questions, we keep the flame of adaptability alive, ensuring that we not only survive but thrive in our ever-changing world

Increased Accountability: Empowering Personal Growth Through Questions

Accountability is the cornerstone of personal growth and self-improvement. It's the act of taking responsibility for our actions and choices, and it's a catalyst for positive change. When it comes to fostering accountability, questions play a pivotal role. They serve as the mirrors that reflect our choices and actions, encouraging us to take ownership of our lives and actively work toward our personal growth.

Self-Reflection as a Tool of Accountability

Self-reflection is the process of examining our thoughts, behaviors, and motivations. It's a form of introspection that allows us to gain insight into our actions and their consequences. Self-reflection often starts with questions. By asking questions like, "Am I living in alignment with my values?" or "What can I do differently to achieve my goals?" we initiate the journey of self-examination and accountability.

Aligning Actions with Values

One of the most powerful ways that questions promote accountability is by helping us align our actions with our values. When we regularly ask, "Am I living in alignment with my values?" we assess whether our daily choices and behaviors reflect what truly matters to us. This question compels us to evaluate whether our actions uphold the principles and beliefs we hold dear.

Owning Your Goals

Accountability extends to goal setting and achievement. Questions like, "What can I do differently to achieve my goals?" prompt us to take a proactive stance toward our objectives. They encourage us to evaluate our progress and make necessary adjustments. By holding ourselves accountable for our goals, we acknowledge our role in shaping our future.

Reflecting on Choices and Consequences

Questions also help us reflect on the consequences of our choices. When we ask, "What impact did my actions have on myself and others?" or "Could I have handled that situation differently?" we take a deeper look at the outcomes of our decisions. This retrospective analysis allows us to learn from our experiences and make more informed choices in the future.

Continuous Improvement

Accountability is a driving force behind continuous improvement. It's the acknowledgment that there is always room for growth and development. By asking questions that assess our actions and decisions, we open the door to personal and professional evolution.

We recognize that we have the power to adapt, learn, and become better versions of ourselves.

Taking Ownership

Ultimately, accountability is about taking ownership of our lives. It's about recognizing that we are the architects of our destinies and that our choices shape our reality. Questions help us navigate this journey of self-ownership. They remind us that personal growth is not a passive process but an active commitment to self-improvement.

Embracing Growth Through Questions

In conclusion, questions are the compass that guides us toward increased accountability and personal growth. They empower us to evaluate our actions, align them with our values, and take ownership of our choices. By consistently asking the right questions, we embark on a transformative journey of self-discovery and improvement. Accountability becomes not just a word but a way of life, leading us toward a brighter and more fulfilling future.

The Power of Positive Thinking: A Journey from Adversity to Triumph

In the heart of Europe, in a land brimming with history and culture, a young student embarked on a transformative journey. Little did he know that his pursuit of education in Belgium would not only test his resilience but also reaffirm the enduring power of positive thinking. This is a story of adversity, determination, and the unwavering belief that positivity can illuminate even the darkest of paths.

A Journey to the Unknown

As the young student set foot in Belgium for his higher education, he was filled with hopes and dreams. It was an exciting new chapter in his life, an opportunity to broaden his horizons and carve a path to a brighter future. However, the journey would soon reveal challenges he had never anticipated.

One of his first experiences in Belgium was securing a part-time job as a dishwasher in a local restaurant. It was a humble beginning, but he approached it with the same enthusiasm that had propelled him across continents. Little did he know that this job would become a crucible in which his character would be tested and his resilience forged.

Going Beyond the Call of Duty

In the bustling kitchen of the restaurant, our protagonist found himself surrounded by diverse colleagues, all working towards a common goal. While the work itself was demanding, he decided to go beyond the call of duty. Each evening, after completing his assigned tasks, while his coworkers hurried to leave, he took it upon himself to ensure the environment was spotless and welcoming for the next day. It was a labor of love, a personal commitment to excellence that transcended his job description.

His intentions were pure. He didn't seek recognition or favor; he believed in the power of positive thinking and the impact of small acts of kindness. However, his actions were misconstrued by his employer. Instead of appreciating his dedication, the employer questioned his motives, accusing him of trying to secure his position or gain favor.

Facing Discrimination and Prejudice

The challenges escalated when our protagonist was burdened with additional tasks after his regular working hours, without additional pay. The situation reached a breaking point when, one day, he could no longer bear the physical and emotional toll of these extra responsibilities. He decided to voice his exhaustion and could not perform the additional tasks.

The response he received was not just disheartening; it was an encounter with discrimination and prejudice. His employer, in a bitter and hurtful tone, reminded him of his ethnicity and made it clear that he was not welcome in the front of the restaurant where patrons dined because "customers don't like black people around."

Resilience and Positive Thinking

Despite the pain and injustice of the moment, our protagonist chose not to succumb to bitterness or despair. He maintained his dignity and composure in the face of prejudice. Little did he know that someone had observed his unwavering dedication and the injustice he faced.

This silent observer recognized the potential and untapped brilliance in our protagonist. He reached out, offering guidance and connections to professionals who could help. This serendipitous encounter led to an opportunity that would change the course of our protagonist's life.

A Path to Redemption and Success

Through the support and mentorship of the compassionate observer, our protagonist secured an opportunity to work for the International Criminal Court as a visiting professional. This opportunity opened doors to a world of exposure and possibilities that he had never imagined. It was a path to redemption, a testament to the enduring power of positive thinking, resilience, and the belief in the potential for change.

In conclusion, this inspirational journey reaffirms the transformative power of positive thinking. It teaches us that adversity can be a stepping stone to greatness. Our protagonist's story is a testament to the resilience of the human spirit and the ability to find light in the darkest of moments. It underscores the importance of practicing positivity and kindness within our environment, regardless of the challenges we face. This remarkable journey from adversity to triumph serves as a beacon of hope and an affirmation that the human spirit can shine even brighter in the face of adversity.

PART I

THE IMPORTANCE OF SELF-REFLECTION

Chapter 2:

The Art of Self-Inquiry

Exploring the Significance of Asking the Right Questions to Oneself

The ability to ask the right questions to oneself is not just a cognitive skill but a powerful tool for personal growth, self-discovery, and problem-solving. It is the art of introspection, a process through which we explore the depths of our thoughts, beliefs, and emotions. In this exploration, we uncover hidden truths, challenge assumptions, and chart a course toward a more meaningful and purposeful life. Let's delve into the significance of asking the right questions to oneself.

Self-Awareness: Asking questions to oneself is the gateway to self-awareness. It's like holding a mirror to your inner world, allowing you to understand your values, motivations, and desires on a deeper level. Questions like, "What truly matters to me?" or "Why do I react this way in certain situations?" prompt self-reflection and foster self-awareness. With self-awareness, you gain clarity about who you are, what you stand for, and what you want to achieve.

Problem-Solving: The significance of asking questions becomes evident when faced with challenges and problems. Instead of dwelling on the issue, you can ask, "What are the possible solutions?" or "What can I learn from this situation?" These questions shift your focus from the problem itself to potential solutions and lessons. They activate your problem-solving abilities and help you navigate adversity with resilience.

Goal Clarity: Aspirations and goals often remain vague until you start asking the right questions. Questions like, "What do I want to achieve in the next five years?" or "What steps can I take to get closer to my goals?" transform abstract dreams into actionable plans. They provide direction, motivation, and a sense of purpose, empowering you to make tangible progress toward your objectives.

Emotional Intelligence: Questions are a tool for exploring your emotional landscape. By asking, "Why do I feel this way?" or "How can I manage my emotions more effectively?" you enhance your emotional intelligence. This self-inquiry enables you to navigate your feelings with greater ease, leading to improved relationships and a healthier emotional well-being.

Personal Growth: The journey of personal growth is paved with questions. It's about constantly asking, "How can I become a better version of myself?" or "What can I learn from my experiences?" This ongoing self-inquiry propels you forward on the path of self-improvement. It encourages you to embrace change, challenge comfort zones, and seek continuous growth.

Decision-Making: Effective decision-making relies on asking the right questions. When facing choices, you can ask, "What are the pros and cons?" or "How does this align with my values?" These questions provide a structured framework for evaluating options and making informed decisions. They minimize impulsivity and reduce the likelihood of regret.

Perspective Shifting: Asking questions allows you to shift your perspective. When confronted with a situation from a single viewpoint, questions like, "What if I looked at this from a different angle?" or "How might others perceive this?" expand your understanding and foster empathy. They promote open-mindedness and collaboration.

Empowerment: The significance of asking questions to oneself lies in empowerment. It empowers you to take control of your life, make intentional choices, and become the author of your own story. Questions are the tools through which you shape your narrative, design your future, and influence your destiny.

In essence, asking the right questions to oneself is an act of self-empowerment and self-discovery. It's a journey inward, a quest for understanding, and a pathway to growth. Through introspection and inquiry, you gain clarity, insight, and the capacity to navigate life's complexities with wisdom and purpose.

Reflection on the Power of Questions for Positive Acts and Proactiveness

Questions have the incredible ability to spark positive actions and Proactiveness in various settings, be it the workplace, team environment, family setting, or shared common spaces. They act as catalysts for self-awareness, problem-solving, and personal growth. Here, we explore examples of powerful questions tailored to these different contexts, designed to inspire positive acts and Proactiveness.

Workplace:

- **"What can I do to improve team collaboration and morale?"** - This question encourages an employee to take proactive steps to foster a more cohesive and productive work environment.
- **"How can I contribute to the company's success beyond my job description?"** - It motivates individuals to seek opportunities to add value and make a meaningful impact.
- **"What innovative solutions can I propose to address ongoing challenges?"** - This question stimulates creative problem-solving and proactive engagement in finding solutions.

Team Environment:

- **"How can I support my teammates to achieve their goals?"** - Encourages team members to be proactive in helping each other succeed.
- **"What can we do to enhance our team's communication and cohesion?"** - Initiates a discussion on proactive measures to strengthen the team dynamic.
- **"What positive behaviors can I model to inspire my team?"** - Promotes leadership through proactive example-setting.

Family Setting:

- **"How can we create a more harmonious and supportive family atmosphere?"** - Encourages family members to actively contribute to a positive home environment.
- **"What small acts of kindness can we perform for each other regularly?"** - Promotes a culture of thoughtfulness and proactive care within the family.
- **"How can we proactively manage conflicts and misunderstandings when they arise?"** - Encourages open communication and proactive conflict resolution strategies.

Common Habitation/Common Area/Shared Space:

- **"What can we collectively do to maintain the cleanliness and orderliness of our shared space?"** - Initiates discussions and actions to ensure a pleasant and proactive shared environment.
- **"How can we proactively reduce our environmental footprint in this shared space?"** - Encourages sustainable practices and responsibility for the shared ecosystem.
- **"What initiatives can we take to build a sense of community and camaraderie among residents?"** -

Promotes proactiveness in fostering a connected and supportive community.

These questions serve as a starting point for positive actions and proactiveness in various settings. They stimulate thought, discussion, and ultimately, inspire individuals and groups to take ownership of their surroundings and contribute positively to their shared spaces and relationships. The power of such questions lies in their ability to engage people in thoughtful reflection and guide them toward proactive behaviors that enhance the quality of life in these diverse contexts.

Chapter 3:

Daily Question Rituals

In the upcoming chapter, 'Daily Question Rituals,' we uncover the profound impact of incorporating intentional self-inquiry into our daily lives. This practice isn't just about asking questions; it's a powerful tool for self-discovery, personal growth, and achieving our goals. Through this chapter, we'll explore how engaging in daily questioning rituals can provide clarity of purpose, enhance self-awareness, and boost our problem-solving abilities. We'll discover how these rituals empower us to navigate life's challenges with resilience and make proactive decisions that align with our values and aspirations. With inspiring examples and practical exercises, we'll embark on a journey to harness the transformative potential of daily questions for a more fulfilling and successful life."

The Benefits of Daily Self-Questioning for Life Fulfillment and Success

Incorporating daily self-questioning into one's routine can be a transformative practice with far-reaching benefits for personal growth, well-being, and success. These questions serve as a compass that guides us through the complexities of life, helping us make informed decisions, maintain focus on our goals, and deepen our self-awareness. Let's delve into the numerous advantages of embracing this daily habit:

Clarity of Purpose: Daily questioning encourages us to reflect on our goals, values, and aspirations. Questions like "What am I working toward?" and "Why is this important to me?" help crystallize our sense of purpose. This clarity empowers us to stay motivated and align our actions with our long-term objectives.

Enhanced Self-Awareness: Self-reflection questions such as "How am I feeling today?" or "What triggered my reactions?" foster self-awareness. By consistently examining our thoughts and emotions, we gain deeper insights into our behaviors and patterns, allowing us to make more conscious choices.

Improved Decision-Making: Daily questions prompt us to evaluate options and make decisions with greater discernment. Queries like "What are the pros and cons?" or "What are my priorities in this situation?" facilitate informed and rational decision-making.

Personal Growth: Self-questioning is a powerful tool for personal development. It encourages us to ask, "What can I learn from today's experiences?" and "How can I grow from challenges?" This mindset of continuous learning and growth propels us forward.

Goal Achievement: Daily self-inquiry keeps us accountable for our goals. Questions like "What steps can I take today to move closer to my objectives?" drive action and progress. They transform aspirations into actionable plans.

Emotional Regulation: Self-questioning helps us manage our emotions effectively. Asking "Why am I feeling this way?" or "How can I respond more constructively?" empowers us to navigate emotional highs and lows with greater resilience.

Stress Reduction: By addressing concerns through questions like "What is causing me stress, and can I control it?" or "What strategies can I use to manage stress?" we gain a sense of control over stressors, reducing their impact on our well-being.

Better Relationships: Daily self-questioning can improve our interactions with others. Questions such as "How can I be more empathetic today?" or "What can I do to strengthen my relationships?" encourage kindness and understanding.

Increased Productivity: Self-inquiry enhances productivity. Questions like "What are my top priorities for the day?" or "How can I make the most of my time?" keep us focused and efficient.

Resilience: Daily questioning builds resilience by fostering a growth mindset. It encourages us to ask, "How can I bounce back from setbacks?" or "What can I learn from failures?" Resilience becomes a natural outcome of this practice.

Enhanced Creativity: Questions stimulate creativity and innovation. When we ask "What if I approached this problem from a different angle?" or "How can I think outside the box?" we invite fresh ideas and solutions.

Gratitude and Positivity: Questions can foster gratitude and a positive mindset. "What am I grateful for today?" or "How can I make today a positive experience?" shift our focus to the brighter aspects of life.

Self-Motivation: Daily self-questioning serves as a self-motivation tool. Questions like "What can I do today to inspire myself?" or "How can I maintain my enthusiasm?" fuel our drive to achieve.

Incorporating daily self-questioning into your routine is like turning on a spotlight that illuminates the path to personal fulfillment and success. It empowers you to navigate life's challenges with resilience, make mindful choices, and cultivate a deeper understanding of yourself and your goals. As you embrace this practice, you'll find that the benefits extend far beyond the questions themselves, enriching every aspect of your life.

Practical Tips and Exercises to Start a Daily Question Practice

Starting a daily question practice can be a transformative step toward personal growth and success. It's a habit that fosters self-awareness, critical thinking, and proactive decision-making. Here are practical tips and exercises to help you initiate and sustain this valuable routine:

Set a Specific Time: Choose a consistent time each day to engage in your question practice. This could be in the morning to set intentions, during a lunch break for reflection, or before bedtime for self-review. Consistency is key.

Create a Quiet Space: Find a peaceful environment where you can focus without distractions. It could be a quiet corner, a cozy chair, or even a park bench. The goal is to create a space conducive to reflection.

Start Simple: Begin with straightforward questions that don't overwhelm you. For example, "What am I grateful for today?" or "What's my main goal for today?" As you build the habit, you can delve into more profound inquiries.

Use Journaling: Many find it helpful to write down their questions and responses in a journal. This not only reinforces the practice but also provides a record of your journey.

Reflect on Your Day: Incorporate questions that review your day. Ask yourself, "What went well today?" and "What could I have done differently?" This self-review aids in continuous improvement.

Explore Different Areas: Cover various aspects of your life with your questions. Include questions related to personal development, relationships, career, health, and any other areas of importance.

Gradually Increase Complexity: As you become more comfortable with the practice, add more complex questions that challenge your thinking. For example, "What limiting beliefs do I need to overcome?" or "How can I make a positive impact on someone's life today?"

Be Open to Uncomfortable Questions: Growth often involves confronting uncomfortable truths. Don't shy away from questions that challenge your beliefs or require self-reflection in difficult areas of your life.

Set Goals: Create a list of goals or intentions for your question practice. For instance, you might aim to enhance self-awareness, improve decision-making, or strengthen your relationships. Having clear objectives can motivate you to stay committed.

Seek Inspiration: Explore books, articles, or podcasts on personal development and self-reflection. They can provide you with new questions to incorporate into your routine.

Share with a Trusted Friend: Consider discussing your daily questions with a trusted friend or mentor. Sharing insights and experiences can deepen your understanding and provide valuable perspectives.

Embrace Consistency Over Perfection: It's normal to miss a day or struggle with certain questions. The key is to stay consistent over time. Don't be too hard on yourself; it's a journey of growth.

Review and Adjust: Periodically assess your question practice. Are your questions still relevant to your goals and aspirations? Adjust them as needed to ensure they align with your evolving needs.

Celebrate Progress: Acknowledge and celebrate the positive changes and insights you gain through your daily questioning. This reinforcement encourages continued growth.

Be Patient: Personal growth is a lifelong journey. Be patient with yourself and remember that the value of practice often becomes more evident as it becomes a natural part of your daily routine.

Starting a daily question practice is an investment in your personal development and success. It's a journey of self-discovery, empowerment, and growth. With dedication and consistency, you'll unlock valuable insights, make more informed decisions, and move steadily toward your aspirations.

PART II:

EMBRACING PROACTIVITY AND PROBLEM-SOLVING

Chapter 4:

Be the Change You Seek

In this Chapter, we delve into the fundamental principle of personal growth and empowerment. It's a reminder that the power to shape our lives, impact our surroundings, and drive positive change ultimately resides within us. This chapter explores the notion that waiting for external circumstances to change is limiting, while taking proactive steps to be the change we seek leads to personal fulfillment, resilience, and meaningful progress. Through inspiring stories, practical insights, and actionable strategies, we illuminate the path to self-empowerment and the transformative impact it can have on our journey toward success and fulfillment."

The Limitations of Waiting for External Change in Life

Waiting for external change to shape our lives can be limiting for several reasons, primarily because it places our fate in the hands of circumstances beyond our control. While external changes and opportunities certainly play a role in our journey, they are often transient and unpredictable. Here's why relying solely on external change can hinder personal growth and success:

1. Lack of Agency: When we wait for external factors to change, we relinquish control over our lives. We become passive observers, dependent on circumstances to determine our direction. This lack of agency can lead to feelings of powerlessness and frustration.

2. Inconsistent and Unpredictable: External changes are often inconsistent and unpredictable. They can be influenced by a multitude of factors, including economic conditions, market trends, and the actions of others. Relying on external change means subjecting our life goals and aspirations to variables beyond our influence.

3. Delayed Progress: Waiting for external change can result in prolonged periods of inaction. Time that could be spent actively pursuing our goals is instead spent in a state of anticipation. This can lead to missed opportunities and hindered personal development.

4. Limited Adaptability: External changes may not always align with our personal goals and values. When we place too much emphasis on these changes, we may find ourselves adapting to circumstances that don't necessarily reflect our true desires and ambitions.

5. Reduced Resilience: Developing resilience and the ability to overcome challenges is essential for personal growth. When we rely solely on external change, we miss out on opportunities to build resilience through adversity and problem-solving.

6. Missed Self-Discovery: Waiting for external change can prevent us from truly understanding ourselves and our capabilities. Personal growth often arises from self-discovery, which is best achieved through proactive action and self-reflection.

7. Limited Personal Transformation: Sustainable and meaningful personal growth usually occurs from within. It involves developing skills, knowledge, and a mindset that empower us to navigate life's challenges effectively. External changes may provide temporary relief, but they rarely lead to lasting transformation.

8. Dependence on Circumstances: Relying on external change perpetuates a cycle of dependency on circumstances to bring us happiness or success. True fulfillment and achievement come from within and are not contingent on external factors.

9. Regret and Missed Opportunities: Waiting for external change can lead to regret in the long run. Many individuals look back and wish they had taken more initiative and control over their lives instead of waiting for the right moment.

10. Stagnation: Ultimately, relying solely on external change can result in a stagnant life. Growth, achievement, and success often require continuous effort, learning, and adaptation. Waiting for external change can lead to complacency and a lack of personal development.

In summary, while external changes and opportunities can certainly play a role in our lives, waiting for them to shape our future can be limiting. True personal growth and success come from within, driven by our goals, actions, and mindset. It's important to proactively pursue our aspirations and be adaptable in the face of external changes rather than passively waiting for them to define our path.

Sharing success stories of some individuals who initiated change.

John Glenn's life is a testament to his remarkable achievements and unwavering dedication to service and exploration. While he is best known as the first American astronaut to orbit Earth in 1962, his success stories extend far beyond this historic milestone.

Pioneering Astronaut: John Glenn's journey to become the first American to orbit the Earth made him a national hero. On February 20, 1962, he piloted the Friendship 7 spacecraft, circling the planet three times in just under five hours. His bravery and accomplishment inspired generations of future astronauts and demonstrated the United States' commitment to space exploration.

Political Career: Glenn's success continued in a different arena when he entered politics. At the age of 53, he embarked on a new chapter as a U.S. Senator from Ohio, a position he held for an impressive 24 years. During his time in the Senate, he was a staunch advocate for various causes, including science, education, and veterans' affairs. His dedication to public service and his constituents earned him respect and admiration across the political spectrum.

Return to Space: Glenn's passion for space exploration never waned. In 1998, at the age of 77, he made history once again by becoming the oldest person to travel in space. His nine-day mission aboard the space shuttle Discovery was a symbol of his enduring commitment to scientific advancement and his belief in the importance of space exploration for future generations.

Educational Legacy: Glenn's impact extended to education. He founded the John Glenn Institute for Public Service and Public Policy at Ohio State University, where he contributed to shaping the minds of young leaders and fostering a sense of civic duty.

Inspiration to All: Beyond his specific accomplishments, John Glenn's life story serves as an inspiration to people of all ages. His courage, determination, and commitment to pushing the boundaries of human knowledge exemplify the spirit of exploration and the pursuit of excellence.

John Glenn's success stories are a testament to his unwavering dedication to the principles of exploration, service, and lifelong learning. He blazed a trail in space, in politics, and in the hearts and minds of those who looked up to him. His legacy continues to inspire individuals to reach for the stars, both figuratively and literally, as they pursue their own dreams and endeavors.

Vera Wang's journey to becoming one of the world's premier women's designers is a testament to her creativity, resilience, and fearless pursuit of her passions. Her success story is both inspiring and a testament to the idea that it's never too late to reinvent oneself.

Early Life and Diverse Interests: Vera Wang's early life was marked by diverse interests and talents. She was a competitive figure skater in her youth and even aspired to make the U.S. Olympic team. Her dedication and discipline from figure skating would later prove invaluable in her fashion career. Wang also worked as a fashion editor at Vogue and a design director at Ralph Lauren, honing her fashion sensibilities.

Entrance into Fashion: What sets Vera Wang apart is her entry into the fashion industry at an age when many would consider it too late for a career change. She transitioned from the world of journalism to fashion design at the age of 40. Her decision to follow her passion and start her own bridal boutique was a bold and risky move.

Innovative Bridal Wear: Vera Wang's bridal designs quickly gained recognition for their unique blend of modernity and classic elegance. She challenged the traditional norms of bridal fashion by introducing non-traditional colors like black and red into her bridal collections. Her innovative designs resonated with brides looking for something distinctive and forward-thinking.

Celebrity Clients and Global Expansion: Wang's exquisite designs earned her a clientele that includes numerous celebrities and prominent figures. Her bridal gowns have been worn by high-profile individuals like Kim Kardashian, Ivanka Trump, and Chelsea Clinton. Wang's success allowed her to expand her brand globally, with boutiques and presence in major fashion capitals worldwide.

Diversification and Brand Extension: Beyond bridal wear, Vera Wang diversified her brand to include ready-to-wear fashion, accessories, fragrances, and even home goods. Her brand became synonymous with luxury, sophistication, and timeless style.

Awards and Recognition: Vera Wang's contributions to the fashion industry have not gone unnoticed. She has received numerous awards and accolades, including the CFDA (Council of Fashion Designers of America) Womenswear Designer of the Year Award. Her impact on bridal fashion has been profound and enduring.

Vera Wang's success story exemplifies the idea that following one's passion and embracing change, even later in life, can lead to remarkable achievements. Her journey from figure skating to journalism and, finally, to fashion design is a testament to the importance of perseverance and staying true to oneself. Wang's ability to redefine bridal fashion and build a global brand serves as an inspiration to aspiring designers and entrepreneurs worldwide.

Dwayne "The Rock" Johnson's remarkable success story is a testament to his unparalleled work ethic, adaptability, and charisma, which have propelled him through multiple career transitions.

Football to Wrestling: Johnson's journey to stardom began as a promising football player. After a brief stint as a backup linebacker for the Canadian Football League's Calgary Stampeders, he made a pivotal decision to leave football behind. At 24, he joined the World Wrestling Federation (WWF). This transition marked the start of his wrestling career, where he adopted the persona "The Rock" and quickly became a fan favorite.

Wrestling Superstar: Dwayne Johnson's wrestling career as "The Rock" was nothing short of legendary. His electrifying presence, charismatic promos, and in-ring talent made him one of the most iconic figures in the history of professional wrestling. He won numerous championships and headlined major events, solidifying his status as a wrestling superstar.

Crossover Success: What sets Johnson apart is his ability to successfully transition from wrestling to the world of entertainment. In the early 2000s, he made a seamless crossover into television and movies. His breakthrough role in "The Scorpion King" (2002) launched his acting career, and he quickly became a sought-after actor in Hollywood.

Blockbuster Movies: Dwayne Johnson's impact on the film industry is undeniable. He has starred in a string of blockbuster movies, including the "Fast and Furious" franchise, "Jumanji: Welcome to the Jungle," and "Moana." His charismatic on-screen presence and versatility have made him one of the highest-paid actors in Hollywood.

Entrepreneurship: Johnson's success extends beyond the entertainment world. He has ventured into entrepreneurship, including launching his own tequila brand, Teremana, and partnering with brands like Under Armour. His business acumen and branding expertise have further diversified his portfolio.

Positive Influence: Beyond his professional achievements, Dwayne Johnson is known for his positive influence and motivational messages. He engages with his fans on social media, sharing personal stories of resilience and hard work. His authenticity and commitment to inspiring others have earned him a devoted following.

Philanthropy: Johnson is also involved in philanthropic endeavors, including supporting children's hospitals and charitable organizations. His commitment to giving back to the community reflects his values of empathy and compassion.

Dwayne "The Rock" Johnson's journey from football to wrestling to Hollywood is a testament to his versatility, adaptability, and relentless pursuit of excellence. His success stories inspire millions around the world to overcome obstacles, reinvent themselves, and chase their dreams with unwavering determination. The Rock's career is a living testament to the idea that with dedication and a never-give-up attitude, one can achieve greatness in multiple fields.

Arnold Schwarzenegger's life is a remarkable journey of resilience, determination, and relentless pursuit of success. He is celebrated for not just one, but two major career transitions that have left an indelible mark on the worlds of bodybuilding, acting, and politics.

Bodybuilding to Acting: Arnold Schwarzenegger's initial career as a bodybuilder was marked by unprecedented success. He became a world champion bodybuilder, winning the prestigious Mr. Olympia title multiple times. His dedication to fitness and bodybuilding became legendary, earning him the nickname "The Austrian Oak."

Transitioning from bodybuilding to acting was a bold move. In his early 30s, Schwarzenegger decided to pursue a career in Hollywood. His imposing physique and charisma set him apart, landing him roles in iconic films like "Conan the Barbarian" (1982) and "The Terminator" (1984). His portrayal of the Terminator in the science fiction franchise catapulted him to international stardom. Schwarzenegger's success as an actor was not only groundbreaking but also a testament to his determination to conquer new frontiers.

Governorship of California: Perhaps the most astonishing career shift in Schwarzenegger's life was when he became the Governor of California in 2003. At the age of 56, he ran for and won the gubernatorial election, serving as the 38th Governor of California from 2003 to 2011.

Schwarzenegger's tenure as governor was marked by his commitment to public service and leadership. He tackled issues such as environmental policy, education reform, and fiscal responsibility. His ability to navigate the complex world of politics demonstrated his adaptability and his dedication to making a difference in the lives of Californians.

Philanthropy and Advocacy: Beyond his careers in bodybuilding, acting, and politics, Schwarzenegger has been actively involved in philanthropic efforts and advocacy. He has been an advocate for fitness and healthy living, promoting physical education programs for children. Additionally, he has been a vocal supporter of environmental causes, emphasizing the importance of sustainability and renewable energy.

Continued Impact: Arnold Schwarzenegger's impact on popular culture, politics, and philanthropy continues to resonate. His life story serves as an inspirational example of the possibilities that come with resilience, hard work, and the courage to embrace new challenges.

Schwarzenegger's success stories are a testament to his remarkable versatility and ability to excel in diverse fields. From bodybuilder to action hero to statesman, he has consistently demonstrated that with unwavering determination, adaptability, and a commitment to making a positive impact, one can achieve greatness in multiple arenas. His life journey inspires others to dream big, work hard, and never stop striving for excellence.

Taikichiro Mori's remarkable success story is a testament to his late-blooming entrepreneurial spirit, astute investments, and relentless pursuit of excellence. Transitioning from academia to real estate, he achieved the extraordinary feat of becoming the richest man in the world in 1992, with a net worth of $13 billion.

Academic Beginnings: Taikichiro Mori began his professional journey as an academic, holding a professorship at Tokyo University. His background in engineering and architecture provided him with a strong foundation in the principles of construction and urban planning.

Entrepreneurial Leap: Mori made a significant career shift at the age of 51 when he founded the Mori Building Company in 1959. This marked the beginning of his venture into real estate investment and development. His decision to enter the world of real estate at a relatively late age was bold and visionary.

Urban Development Visionary: Mori's brilliance lay in his ability to foresee the potential of urban development, particularly in Tokyo. During a period of rapid economic growth in Japan, he recognized the increasing demand for office space and residential properties in the bustling metropolis.

Strategic Investments: Mori's investments in prime real estate locations in Tokyo, including the prestigious Roppongi Hills district, proved to be masterful. He focused on constructing high-rise buildings and mixed-use developments, capitalizing on the limited available land in the city.

Richest Man in the World: By the early 1990s, Mori's real estate investments had yielded tremendous returns. In 1992, he achieved the distinction of being the richest man in the world, with a net worth of $13 billion, surpassing even well-known global billionaires.

Legacy in Urban Development: Mori's legacy extends beyond his financial success. He played a pivotal role in transforming the Tokyo skyline and contributing to the city's modernization. His developments, such as Roppongi Hills, set new standards for urban planning and architectural innovation.

Philanthropic Endeavors: Taikichiro Mori was also known for his philanthropic activities. He supported various educational and cultural initiatives, further contributing to the betterment of society.

Taikichiro Mori's success story exemplifies the power of vision, calculated risk-taking, and adaptability. His ability to identify and seize opportunities in the real estate market, even after a career in academia, highlights the importance of recognizing one's strengths and pursuing one's passions.

Mori's enduring impact on the urban landscape of Tokyo and his extraordinary financial success serve as an inspiration to aspiring entrepreneurs and investors worldwide. His legacy as a late-blooming real estate magnate and philanthropist continues to influence the worlds of business, urban development, and philanthropy, reminding us that success knows no age limit when fueled by passion and strategic vision.

Chapter 5:

Opportunities in Problem-Solving

In Chapter 5, 'Opportunities in Problem-Solving,' we embark on a transformative exploration of how challenges and obstacles can become the breeding ground for opportunities and growth. Just as adversity can inspire, problems and difficulties can trigger innovative thinking, personal development, and the discovery of untapped potential. Within this chapter, we uncover the profound ways in which effective problem-solving can lead to innovation, market differentiation, personal and professional advancement, and even the creation of businesses that address unmet needs. It's a journey that illustrates how a positive mindset and a strategic approach to challenges can turn stumbling blocks into steppingstones toward a brighter future."

Opportunities in Problem-Solving: Turning Challenges into Success

The saying "inspiration can come from condolence visits" is a poignant reminder that even in moments of grief and adversity, there can be sources of inspiration and growth. Similarly, in the realm of problem-solving, challenges and obstacles can serve as fertile ground for opportunities to flourish. Here, we explore the concept of opportunities in problem-solving and how tackling difficulties with a positive mindset can lead to transformative outcomes.

Catalyst for Innovation: Problems and obstacles stimulate creative thinking and innovation. When faced with a challenge, individuals and organizations are prompted to explore new solutions, technologies, and approaches. This innovative mindset can lead to the development of groundbreaking products, services, or processes that not only address the initial problem but also create new opportunities within the market.

Market Needs and Niche Discovery: Problems often signify unmet needs or gaps in the market. Identifying these needs and addressing them through problem-solving can result in the creation of products or services that cater to a specific niche. This can lead to market differentiation and the establishment of a unique competitive advantage.

Personal Growth and Skill Development: Overcoming obstacles requires individuals to acquire new skills, expand their knowledge, and enhance their problem-solving abilities. These personal development efforts can open doors to opportunities that were previously out of reach. For example, acquiring proficiency in a particular technology to solve a business challenge may lead to a lucrative career in that field.

Resilience and Adaptability: Successfully navigating challenges builds resilience and adaptability. Individuals and organizations that learn how to overcome obstacles are better equipped to thrive in a constantly changing environment. This adaptability can lead to seizing unforeseen opportunities and staying ahead in highly competitive industries.

Networking and Collaboration: Problem-solving often involves collaboration with others, whether within a team or through partnerships. Building a network of professionals and experts in various fields can lead to unexpected opportunities. These connections may result in joint ventures, mentorship opportunities, or access to valuable resources.

Entrepreneurship and Startups: Many successful startups are born out of entrepreneurs identifying problems and providing innovative solutions. Entrepreneurs are problem-solvers by nature, and their ability to recognize market gaps and address them can lead to the creation of thriving businesses.

Social Impact and Change: Addressing societal problems can lead to opportunities for positive change and social impact. Individuals and organizations that focus on solving social, environmental, or humanitarian challenges can create meaningful opportunities to make a difference in the world.

Continuous Improvement: Embracing a problem-solving mindset encourages a culture of continuous improvement within organizations. This commitment to ongoing refinement can result in increased efficiency, cost savings, and enhanced competitiveness.

Infact, problems and obstacles should not be viewed solely as roadblocks but as potential sources of opportunities. The act of problem-solving, when approached with a positive and proactive mindset, can lead to transformative outcomes. It's a reminder that challenges, while daunting, can also serve as catalysts for growth, innovation, and success. By recognizing the inherent opportunities in problem-solving, individuals and organizations can navigate adversity with confidence, resilience, and the anticipation of brighter horizons.

The Power of Problem-Solving: Attracting Opportunities and Defining Values

Problem-solving is the crucible through which our values, significance, and worth are forged. In the grand tapestry of life, the ability to tackle and overcome challenges at every level is not just a skill but a defining characteristic of who we are. It is through the lens of problem-solving that we attract opportunities, shape our destinies, and reveal the true essence of our character.

Opportunities as Solutions: Every problem presents an opportunity in disguise. When we confront challenges head-on, we become solution architects, crafting innovative answers to complex questions. This problem-solving prowess, whether in our personal lives or professional endeavors, is like a magnet that attracts opportunities. People and organizations seek problem-solvers because they recognize the value of those who can navigate uncertainty and transform obstacles into steppingstones.

Skill Enhancement: Problem-solving is a skill that transcends specific challenges. It's a dynamic ability that, when honed, enhances our adaptability, resilience, and versatility. As we refine our problem-solving toolkit, we become more valuable contributors in our workplaces and communities. This expertise paves the way for personal and professional growth, as individuals who can effectively address issues are often entrusted with more significant responsibilities and leadership roles.

Innovation and Entrepreneurship: Some of the world's most successful businesses and ventures were born out of a quest to solve problems. Entrepreneurs identify market gaps and develop innovative solutions that not only address those issues but also create entirely new opportunities. This entrepreneurial spirit is fueled by the belief that problems are not roadblocks but pathways to prosperity.

Values and Integrity: Problem-solving goes beyond practicality; it reveals our values and integrity. How we approach and resolve challenges speaks volumes about our ethics, determination, and commitment to making a positive impact. Those who consistently demonstrate the ability to solve problems with integrity earn the trust and respect of others, opening doors to collaborations, partnerships, and leadership roles.

Self-Discovery: The journey of problem-solving is a profound path of self-discovery. As we navigate challenges, we uncover hidden strengths, confront weaknesses, and gain a deeper understanding of our capabilities. This self-awareness empowers us to make choices that align with our values and aspirations, attracting opportunities that resonate with our authentic selves.

A Life of Significance: In the grand tapestry of existence, a life devoid of problem-solving is like a blank canvas. It is through challenges and their resolutions that we paint the vivid strokes of a life rich in meaning and significance. Opportunities are drawn to individuals who actively engage with the world, tackle its complexities, and leave a lasting impact through their contributions.

Finally, problem-solving is not merely a practical skill but a defining aspect of our identities. It is the force that attracts opportunities and shapes the trajectory of our lives. Through our ability to confront and conquer challenges, we infuse value into our existence, leaving an indelible mark on the world. As we embrace problem-solving as a cornerstone of our journey, we unlock doors to a future brimming with purpose, growth, and enduring significance.

Albert Einstein's life is replete with examples of how he turned challenges into opportunities, demonstrating that adversity and unconventional thinking can lead to groundbreaking discoveries. Here are a few real-life instances that showcase Einstein's remarkable ability to transform difficulties into opportunities:

Late Speech Development: As a child, Einstein didn't speak until he was four years old. This delayed speech development might have seemed like a hindrance, but it allowed him to observe the world in a unique way. His introspective nature and the time he spent silently contemplating the universe would later contribute to his groundbreaking theories in physics.

Abstract Questioning: Einstein's propensity to ask abstract and unconventional questions puzzled his elementary school teachers. While it might have made him appear lazy to some, this inquisitive nature was the foundation of his future scientific inquiries. His ability to question fundamental assumptions in physics led to the development of the theory of relativity.

Rejection from College: After completing his secondary education, Einstein applied to the Polytechnic Institute in Zurich but failed the entrance exam. Undeterred, he attended a preparatory school and retook the exam the following year, eventually gaining admission. This setback, which could have discouraged him, instead motivated him to prove his worth.

Clerk at a Patent Office: After graduating from college, Einstein struggled to secure an academic position. He worked as a patent examiner at the Swiss Patent Office in Bern. This seemingly ordinary job provided him with ample time to think and explore his own ideas. It was during this period that he developed many of his groundbreaking theories, including the theory of special relativity.

$E=mc^2$ and Nobel Prize: Einstein's theory of relativity, particularly the famous equation $E=mc^2$, revolutionized our understanding of the universe. Despite the initially controversial nature of his work, he was eventually awarded the Nobel Prize in Physics in 1921 for his explanation of the photoelectric effect, another groundbreaking contribution.

Exile and Legacy: Einstein, a Jewish scientist, faced persecution during World War II due to his heritage and his outspoken stance against nuclear weapons. He fled Nazi Germany and settled in the United States. This exile allowed him to collaborate with other brilliant minds and contribute to the Manhattan Project, which ultimately led to the development of atomic weapons. After the war, Einstein continued to advocate for peace and civil rights, leaving a legacy beyond his scientific contributions.

Albert Einstein's life serves as a testament to the power of resilience, unconventional thinking, and the ability to turn challenges into opportunities. His remarkable journey from a speech-delayed child to a scientific genius reshaped our understanding of the universe. Einstein's story encourages us to embrace adversity, question the status quo, and seek opportunities even in the face of obstacles. It reminds us that challenges can be steppingstones to greatness when approached with determination and an unwavering spirit of curiosity.

Part III:

Cultivating an Opportunity Mindset

In this section: Cultivating an Opportunity Mindset,' we delve deep into the art of embracing opportunities with open arms, fostering a perspective that sees potential in every challenge. This section is a transformative journey that explores the mindset shifts, strategies, and habits needed to harness the power of opportunities. From reframing adversity as a launching pad for growth to developing proactive habits that attract success, Part 3 is a guide to cultivating an opportunity-centric approach to life and achieving greater personal and professional fulfillment."

Chapter 6:

Unleashing Your Potential: The Power of Personal Daily Questions

Pascal Mercier's contemplative words remind us that within each of us lies an abundance of untapped potential. While human experience allows us to access only a fraction of our innate abilities, the journey to unleash the rest begins with a simple yet profound practice: personal daily questions. These questions serve as the key to unlocking the rich, valuable, and often dormant resources hidden within us, as highlighted by Blake Roney and Myles Munroe.

Self-Reflection and Awareness: Personal daily questions act as a compass for self-reflection and self-awareness. They encourage us to pause and delve deep within ourselves, asking probing questions like, "What am I truly passionate about?" or "What are my unique strengths?" These questions prompt us to explore our inner landscape, identify our core values, and recognize our latent talents. In this process of self-discovery, we unveil the potential that has been waiting patiently within us.

Goal Clarity: Daily questions help us gain clarity about our aspirations and goals. By asking questions such as, "What do I want to achieve today?" or "What steps can I take toward my long-term objectives?" we set a clear direction for our actions. This focus on goal-oriented questions allows us to channel our untapped potential toward meaningful endeavors and ensures that our daily efforts align with our larger life purpose.

Problem-Solving and Creativity: The act of daily questioning stimulates our problem-solving abilities and creative thinking. When we ask ourselves, "How can I overcome this challenge?" or "What innovative solutions can I explore?" we activate our cognitive processes and tap into our reservoir of creativity. This constant exercise of problem-solving and ideation awakens the dormant potential for ingenious solutions and fresh perspectives.

Personal Growth: Personal daily questions foster a growth mindset, encouraging us to continuously improve. Questions like, "What can I learn from today's experiences?" or "How can I become a better version of myself?" propel us toward personal development. This commitment to growth unearths our untapped potential, as it motivates us to acquire new skills, broaden our knowledge, and evolve as individuals.

Positive Mindset: Daily questions can be framed to promote a positive mindset. By asking questions like, "What am I grateful for today?" or "How can I spread positivity to others?" We shift our focus toward the brighter aspects of life. This positive outlook not only enhances our well-being but also unlocks our potential to radiate optimism, inspire others, and make a meaningful impact.

Accountability and Action: Personal daily questions hold us accountable for our actions and choices. When we regularly ask questions such as, "Am I living in alignment with my values?" or "What can I do differently to achieve my goals?" we take ownership of our lives. This proactive stance ensures that our untapped potential is not dormant but actively harnessed to drive purposeful action.

In the eloquent words of Blake Roney and Myles Munroe, the untapped potential within us is a valuable resource waiting to be deployed. Personal daily questions serve as the catalyst for this deployment, guiding us on a transformative journey of self-discovery, growth, and purposeful action. They enable us to unlock the treasures hidden within and, in turn, bless the world with the richness of our unique abilities, ultimately realizing the profound potential that resides within each of us.

Personal Growth: The Crucible of Leadership and Potential Realization

The analogy "Leadership is not something that is done to people, like fixing your teeth" underscores the profound truth that leadership is not a passive act but a dynamic, self-directed journey. It's a journey deeply intertwined with personal growth, as enhancing one's potential and becoming an effective leader are intrinsically linked. Here's how personal growth serves as the crucible for both potential realization and leadership development:

Self-Awareness as the Foundation: Leadership begins with self-awareness, and personal growth is its cornerstone. Leaders who understand their strengths, weaknesses, values, and aspirations are better equipped to lead authentically. Personal growth encourages introspection through questions like, "Who am I?" and "What do I stand for?" These inquiries deepen self-awareness, which is essential for effective leadership.

Expanding Capacities: Personal growth expands one's capacities, nurturing the potential for leadership. Through continuous learning, skill development, and emotional intelligence cultivation, individuals become better equipped to handle the complexities of leadership. As they broaden their knowledge and skill sets, they unlock the potential to lead with competence and confidence.

Resilience and Adaptability: Leadership often demands resilience and adaptability. Personal growth equips individuals with the emotional resilience to withstand challenges and the adaptability to thrive in changing environments. It encourages them to ask questions like, "How can I bounce back from setbacks?" and "How can I embrace change?" These questions fortify their leadership potential.

Empathy and Relationship Building: Effective leaders excel in interpersonal skills and relationship building. Personal growth fosters empathy and enhances the ability to connect with others on a profound level. Leaders who ask questions like, "How can I understand others' perspectives?" and "How can I build trust and rapport?" unlock their potential to lead with empathy and influence.

Vision and Purpose: Leadership often hinges on a compelling vision and a sense of purpose. Personal growth encourages individuals to ponder questions like, "What is my vision for the future?" and "What legacy do I want to leave?" As they clarify their purpose and vision, they unearth their leadership potential, inspiring others to follow a meaningful path.

Lifelong Learning: Leaders are lifelong learners, constantly seeking to improve. Personal growth instills a commitment to continuous self-improvement through questions like, "What can I learn from this experience?" and "How can I become a better leader?" Leaders who embody this mindset continually realize their potential and inspire others to do the same.

Leading by Example: Authentic leadership is rooted in leading by example. Personal growth encourages individuals to align their values with their actions, embodying the principles they stand for. Leaders who ask, "Am I walking the talk?" and "How can I set a positive example?" not only enhance their potential but also inspire others through their authenticity.

Transformative Leadership: True leadership transcends mere management; it involves inspiring and transforming others. Personal growth unlocks the potential for transformative leadership by fostering a sense of purpose, vision, and an unwavering commitment to positive change.

In essence, leadership and personal growth are intertwined on a profound level. Personal growth is not a destination but a continuous journey of self-discovery, skill enhancement, and character development. As individuals embark on this journey, they unlock their potential, and their leadership capabilities naturally evolve. By embracing personal growth, they become not just leaders who drive change but also catalysts for the growth and potential realization of those they lead

Self-Reflection Journal:
- Start a journal dedicated to self-reflection.
- Regularly jot down moments when you felt truly engaged, fulfilled, or excited.
- Describe the activities, tasks, or circumstances that led to those feelings.
- Note any skills or talents you believe were at play during those moments.
- Over time, patterns may emerge that reveal your passions and strengths.

Strengths Assessment:
- Take a strengths assessment or quiz, such as the Gallup StrengthsFinder or VIA Character Strengths survey.
- These assessments provide insights into your natural talents and strengths.
- Analyze the results to identify patterns and recurring themes.
- Consider how these strengths align with your interests and passions.

Seek Feedback:
- Reach out to friends, family, colleagues, and mentors.
- Ask them what they believe are your strengths and what activities or topics ignite your enthusiasm.
- External perspectives can provide valuable insights.

Passion Projects:

- Start a small project or hobby related to something you're curious or passionate about.
- Engage in the activity consistently for a few weeks or months.
- Pay attention to how you feel while working on it.
- If you find yourself excited and immersed, it might indicate a passion or strength.

Goal Setting:

- Create a list of short-term and long-term goals.
- Consider which goals genuinely excite you and make you eager to work on them.
- Goals that align with your passions are likely to utilize your strengths.

Childhood Interests:

- Reflect on what activities or interests you were naturally drawn to as a child.
- Often, our childhood inclinations can offer clues about our enduring passions and talents.

Take Courses or Workshops:

- Enroll in courses or workshops on a variety of topics.
- Experiment with different subjects to see which ones captivate your interest.
- It can lead you to discover new passions and strengths.

Networking and Volunteering:

- Attend networking events or volunteer for different causes.
- Engaging in diverse activities can expose you to new experiences and interests.
- Observe what resonates with you during these interactions.

Mind Mapping:

- Create a mind map with "Passions" or "Strengths" at the center.

- Branch out with related interests, skills, and experiences.
- Visualizing these connections can provide clarity.

Consider using professional assessments like the Myers-Briggs Type Indicator (MBTI) or the Enneagram. These tools can offer insights into your personality traits and tendencies, helping you identify your strengths and passions.

Chapter 7:

Creating Positive Change

Life is a canvas waiting for your creative brush strokes, and change is the vibrant palette from which you draw your inspiration. In the tapestry of existence, the ability to instigate positive change is the thread that weaves the most profound stories of personal growth and societal transformation. This chapter explores the art and science of creating positive change in our lives and the world around us. It delves into the principles, strategies, and mindset shifts that empower individuals to be the architects of their destiny and champions of progress. As we journey through these pages, we'll uncover the transformative potential of daily questions as catalysts for change, and we'll witness how small, intentional acts can ripple into waves of impact. So, let us embark on this exploration of creativity and change, embracing the profound truth that lies in every question the power to shape a brighter tomorrow.

The Concept of True Wealth: Beyond the Pocket, into the Heart

In a world that often measures wealth in material possessions, financial success, and tangible assets, it's essential to recognize that true wealth extends far beyond the contents of one's pocket. Karl Popper's poignant words about tolerance allude to a profound concept: the idea that genuine wealth resides within the heart and soul of an individual, manifested through patience and tolerance towards others.

Wealth of Character: True wealth encompasses the richness of character and the depth of one's values. It is not merely about accumulating material possessions but about nurturing qualities like empathy, compassion, kindness, and understanding. When a person embraces tolerance, they enrich their character and elevate their moral and ethical wealth.

Emotional Wealth: Emotional wealth, often overlooked in the pursuit of material gain, is an integral component of true prosperity. An individual who practices patience and tolerance cultivates emotional resilience and fortitude. They are better equipped to navigate life's challenges and maintain mental well-being.

Interpersonal Wealth: In the realm of relationships, tolerance and patience are currency. A person who extends these qualities fosters deeper connections with others. They create an environment of trust, respect, and harmony, which, in turn, enriches their interpersonal wealth.

Community and Societal Wealth: True wealth extends beyond the individual to the community and society at large. When people collectively practice tolerance and patience, they contribute to the creation of inclusive, diverse, and harmonious communities. This social wealth is immeasurable in its positive impact.

Spiritual Fulfillment: Beyond the material world, there exists a realm of spiritual wealth. For many, the act of tolerance and patience aligns with their spiritual beliefs and brings them a sense of purpose and fulfillment.

Global Prosperity: On a global scale, true wealth is reflected in the ability to foster peace, cooperation, and understanding among nations and cultures. The world becomes richer when nations practice tolerance, transcending borders and forging bonds of unity.

In essence, true wealth is a holistic concept that encompasses personal, emotional, interpersonal, and societal dimensions. It is built on a foundation of patience and tolerance, two virtues that enable individuals and societies to coexist harmoniously and thrive collectively. As Karl Popper suggested, claiming the right not to tolerate the intolerant is an essential defense of a tolerant society. It is through the practice of these virtues that we discover that the most valuable treasures are not found in our pockets but reside deep within our hearts and souls.

Creating positive change in one's environment is a noble pursuit that can have a lasting impact. Here are strategies for using your resources to bring about positive change: **Identify Your Resources:**

Begin by taking inventory of your resources. These can include financial assets, time, skills, knowledge, networks, and personal influence. Understanding what you have at your disposal is the first step.

Define Your Values and Goals:

Clarify your values and determine the specific positive changes you want to make in your environment. Whether it's improving education, environmental sustainability, community development, or other causes, having clear goals is crucial.

Educate Yourself:

Invest time in learning about the issues or causes you are passionate about. Knowledge is a powerful resource. Stay informed about the latest developments, challenges, and opportunities in your chosen field.

Volunteer and Collaborate:

Seek out local organizations, nonprofits, or community groups aligned with your goals. Volunteering your time and skills can be a valuable resource. Collaborating with like-minded individuals and organizations can amplify your impact.

Donate Financially:

Financial resources can be a significant driver of positive change. Consider allocating a portion of your income to support causes you care about. Regular donations, one-time contributions, or setting up a charitable fund can all make a difference.

Mentorship and Skill Sharing:

If you possess specific skills or knowledge, consider mentoring others or offering workshops to share your expertise. Empowering others with your resources can lead to sustainable change.

Engage in Advocacy:

Use your voice and influence to advocate for change. Write letters to policymakers, participate in advocacy campaigns, or join grassroots movements that align with your values.

Be Mindful of Your Environmental Impact:

Make conscious choices to reduce your environmental footprint. This can include reducing waste, conserving energy, supporting eco-friendly products, and advocating for sustainable practices in your community.

Support Local Initiatives:

Invest in your local community by supporting small businesses, local artisans, and community projects. Your resources can help foster economic growth and stability in your area.

Start Your Initiative:

If you identify a gap in addressing an issue you are passionate about, consider starting your initiative or nonprofit organization.

Many grassroots movements and nonprofits began with the vision and dedication of individuals like you.

Use Technology and social media

Leverage technology and social media platforms to raise awareness about your cause and mobilize support. Engage with a wider audience and connect with like-minded individuals globally.

Measure and Adjust:

Regularly evaluate the impact of your efforts. Collect data, solicit feedback, and be willing to adapt your strategies as needed to maximize positive change.

Lead by Example:

Be a role model for the change you wish to see. Your actions and commitment can inspire others to join the cause.

Remember that creating positive change is an ongoing journey. It requires dedication, persistence, and collaboration with others who share your vision. By effectively leveraging your resources and staying committed to your goals, you can make a meaningful impact on your environment and contribute to a better world.

PART IV:
INSPIRING ACTION AND TRANSFORMATION

Chapter 8:

From Craving to Contentment

Introduction to Chapter 8: From Craving to Contentment

In the hustle and bustle of modern life, it's all too easy to fall into the trap of constantly craving more — more success, more wealth, more recognition. Yet, as we navigate this relentless pursuit, we often discover that genuine contentment remains elusive. Chapter 8 of our journey delves deep into the concept of contentment, exploring how the incessant desire for more can be a roadblock to true fulfillment. It invites us to pause, reflect, and embrace the profound wisdom that contentment is not found in accumulating possessions or status but in appreciating what we already have. Through the lens of daily questions, we'll explore how asking the right inquiries can lead us from the tumultuous sea of craving to the tranquil harbor of contentment. So, let us embark on this transformative exploration, learning to savor the richness of the present moment and finding contentment amid the clamor of desires.

In a world that often emphasizes the pursuit of more — more wealth, more success, more possessions — the concept of contentment may appear elusive. However, the timeless wisdom that contentment comes from embracing what one has holds a profound truth that transcends materialism. In this exploration, we will delve deep into the idea that contentment is not an elusive destination but a state of being that can be cultivated by appreciating and embracing the abundance already present in our lives.

The Paradox of Desire: The Pursuit of More

The human condition is characterized by desires and ambitions. From a young age, we are encouraged to dream big, set goals, and strive for success. This ambition, while driving progress and innovation, often leads to a paradoxical state of perpetual desire. As we achieve one goal, another takes its place, creating a never-ending cycle of craving. This phenomenon is rooted in the belief that fulfillment is contingent on external acquisitions, a notion perpetuated by societal norms and consumer culture.

The Illusion of External Fulfillment: Chasing Shadows

Many individuals embark on a relentless quest for external validation and possessions, believing that these acquisitions will bring them happiness and contentment. They accumulate wealth, prestige, and possessions in the pursuit of a fleeting sense of accomplishment. Yet, the joy derived from these external trappings is often short-lived, leaving individuals yearning for the next acquisition, the next milestone, or the next achievement.

The Hedonic Treadmill: A Vicious Cycle

Psychologists have coined the term "hedonic treadmill" to describe the phenomenon where individuals constantly adapt to improved circumstances, leading to a baseline level of happiness. As they accumulate more, their expectations rise in tandem, resulting in a perpetual chase for the elusive "more" that promises happiness but remains just out of reach. This treadmill keeps individuals in a state of perpetual dissatisfaction, preventing them from experiencing contentment.

The Art of Gratitude: Embracing the Present Moment

Contentment, however, resides not in the future but in the present moment. It is the art of finding fulfillment in the here and now, appreciating the beauty of existence as it unfolds. Gratitude is the key that unlocks the door to this profound state of being. When individuals shift their focus from what they lack to what they have, they embark on a transformative journey toward contentment.

Cultivating Gratitude: A Daily Practice

Gratitude is not a passive state but an active practice that can be cultivated. One powerful way to do this is through the daily practice of asking the right questions. By intentionally directing our inquiries toward the abundance in our lives, we begin to unearth the treasures hidden in plain sight. Questions like, "What am I grateful for today?" or "What moments brought me joy?" prompt us to reflect on the beauty, kindness, and love that surround us daily.

The Ripple Effect of Contentment: Impact on Well-being

Contentment is not a solitary experience; it has a profound impact on overall well-being. Studies have shown that individuals who regularly practice gratitude and embrace what they have experience improved mental health, reduced stress levels, enhanced relationships, and increased life satisfaction. This ripple effect extends beyond the individual to positively influence the community and society as a whole.

Contentment and Relationships: The Power of Presence

In the pursuit of external goals, individuals often neglect the quality of their relationships. However, contentment fosters a deeper sense of presence and connection with loved ones. When we appreciate the people in our lives and the moments we share with them, we enhance the quality of our relationships, nurturing bonds that bring genuine fulfillment.

The Art of Letting Go: Releasing the Clutter

Contentment is also intertwined with the art of letting go. As individuals embrace what they have, they may realize that many possessions and pursuits no longer align with their values or bring true joy. Letting go of excess and clutter liberates space and energy for the things that genuinely matter, creating a sense of lightness and freedom.

The Role of Mindfulness: Present-Centered Awareness

Mindfulness practices, such as meditation and mindful breathing, play a significant role in cultivating contentment. These practices train individuals to be present in each moment, fully experiencing the richness of life as it unfolds. Through mindfulness, individuals learn to let go of the past and future, finding contentment in the present-centered awareness of the now.

The Art of Contentment in Adversity: Resilience and Strength

True contentment is not contingent on external circumstances but can be found even in adversity. Individuals who embrace what they have, even when facing challenges, demonstrate resilience and inner strength. They find solace in the knowledge that, regardless of external circumstances, they possess the inner resources to navigate life's ups and downs.

Transcending the Ego: From Self-Centered Desires to Selfless Giving

Contentment also involves a shift from self-centered desires to selfless giving. When individuals appreciate the abundance in their lives, they are more inclined to share their blessings with others. Acts of kindness, generosity, and compassion become a natural expression of their contentment, creating a positive impact in their communities.

The Art of Contentment: Embracing What You Have

In a world that often celebrates the pursuit of more—more wealth, more possessions, more success—it's easy to overlook one of life's most profound truths: contentment is not a destination reached through accumulation but a state of being cultivated by embracing what you have. In this exploration of contentment, we will journey through the art of appreciating the present, understanding the roots of discontent, and discovering how daily questions can be powerful guides on this transformative path.

The Elusive Nature of Contentment

Contentment is often likened to a rare jewel, sought after by many but discovered by few. It is an elusive state of being that seems to shimmer just out of reach, even as we strive to grasp it. The irony lies in the fact that while society often teaches us to measure our worth by external markers of success—our bank account, possessions, and achievements—true contentment resides within, waiting to be unlocked.

The Role of Gratitude

At the heart of contentment lies gratitude, the art of acknowledging and appreciating the blessings, big and small, that grace our lives. Gratitude shifts our focus from what we lack to what we possess. It invites us to savor the richness of the present moment, recognizing that happiness is not contingent on future acquisitions but on the appreciation of the here and now.

Embracing gratitude is akin to turning on a light in the dark room of desire. It illuminates the treasures already present in our lives, whether it's the warmth of a loving relationship, the beauty of a sunset, or the simple pleasure of a shared meal with friends. When we cultivate gratitude through daily practices like journaling or meditation, we train our minds to seek the beauty and abundance that surrounds us.

The Roots of Discontent

To truly understand contentment, we must also examine the roots of discontent. What drives our relentless pursuit of more? It often springs from societal pressures and messages that equate success with accumulation. We are bombarded with advertisements that tell us we need the latest gadgets, fashion, or status symbols to be happy. These messages fuel a cycle of desire, making us believe that contentment is just one purchase away.

Moreover, the human mind has a remarkable ability to adapt to new circumstances. This adaptability, while a valuable survival mechanism, can also lead to a phenomenon known as the "hedonic treadmill." This treadmill suggests that as we acquire more, our expectations and desires also rise, and we become accustomed to our improved circumstances. As a result, we may find ourselves in a perpetual chase for the next source of pleasure or satisfaction, mistakenly believing that it will bring lasting contentment.

The Power of Daily Questions in Cultivating Contentment

Daily questions are like compasses guiding us through the terrain of our thoughts and emotions. They can play a transformative role in helping us embrace what we have and find contentment. Here are some key ways in which daily questions can be harnessed for this purpose:

1. Shifting Focus:

- Daily questions prompt us to shift our focus from what we lack to what we have. Questions like, "What am I grateful for today?" encourage us to recognize the abundance in our lives, no matter how small or seemingly ordinary.

2. Reflection and Perspective:

- Questions provide an opportunity for self-reflection and perspective. By asking, "What truly matters to me?" we gain insight into our core values and priorities. This awareness can guide us toward decisions and actions aligned with our deepest desires.

3. Mindfulness and Presence:

- Daily questions invite us to be present in the moment. When we ask, "How can I savor today's experiences?" we become more attuned to the beauty and richness of each moment, rather than rushing past it in pursuit of the next goal.

4. Breaking the Cycle:

- Questions can disrupt the cycle of desire and craving. When we inquire, "Do I really need this, or do I already have enough?" we challenge the automatic impulse to accumulate and encourage a more mindful approach to consumption.

5. Tracking Progress:

Daily questions serve as a tool for tracking our progress on the journey toward contentment. We can ask, "How have I grown in embracing what I have?" This reflection reinforces positive habits and reinforces our commitment to contentment.

Embracing Contentment in Practice

Contentment is not a passive state but an active choice. It requires intentional practice and a shift in mindset. Here are some practical steps to embrace contentment in your daily life:

1. Gratitude Journaling:

Dedicate time each day to jot down three things you're grateful for. These can be simple pleasures, meaningful relationships, or personal achievements. Over time, you'll build a repository of positive moments to revisit whenever you need a reminder of your blessings.

2. Mindful Consumption:

Before making a purchase, pause and ask yourself whether it aligns with your true needs and values. Avoid impulse buying and consider the long-term impact of your choices on your contentment.

In a world fixated on the pursuit of more, contentment is a precious gem waiting to be discovered within. It is not a destination but a journey, a state of being that can be cultivated through the daily practice of gratitude, mindfulness, and the embrace of what one has. When individuals shift their focus from the external to the internal, from craving to contentment, they unlock a profound sense of fulfillment that enriches their lives and radiates positivity to those around them. The path to true contentment begins with the realization that, indeed, the richest treasures are already within our grasp.

Fulfillment: The Gift of Helping Others

In a world often driven by personal success and individual accomplishments, the profound truth that fulfillment comes from helping others shines as a guiding light. Stories of ordinary people who found extraordinary fulfillment by extending a helping hand to those in need echo the timeless wisdom of luminaries like Tony Robbins, Albert Einstein, and Rod Stryker. These stories remind us that success without fulfillment is an empty pursuit, and the deepest sense of purpose is discovered in the act of serving others.

Bryan Anderson: The Roadside Samaritan

Bryan Anderson's story is one that epitomizes the essence of selfless service. A chance encounter with a stranded old lady on the side of the road became the catalyst for a chain of love and kindness. Bryan, despite his humble appearance, stopped to assist the distressed woman. He not only changed her flat tire but also reassured her with a warm smile. In return, he asked for a simple yet profound gesture: to pay forward the kindness to someone else in need. Bryan understood that true fulfillment lay in the continuation of this chain of love.

The Pregnant Waitress: A Surprise Gift of Generosity

In a small, dimly lit cafe, another tale of generosity and fulfillment unfolded. A pregnant waitress, working tirelessly to support her growing family, exemplified the spirit of giving. Despite her own struggles, she wore a sweet and friendly smile, serving patrons with a warm heart. When a kind-hearted lady, inspired by Bryan's example, visited the cafe, she left a significant gift behind. A hundred-dollar bill became the conduit for a message of love and compassion.

The pregnant waitress, unaware of the true identity of her generous benefactor, was deeply moved by the stranger's kindness. The unexpected financial assistance touched her heart and eased her worries about the impending arrival of her child. She felt the impact of the chain of love, realizing that a single act of kindness could set off a series of transformative events.

Fulfillment Beyond Material Wealth

Albert Einstein's words resonate in these stories: "A life directed chiefly toward the fulfillment of personal desires will sooner or later always lead to bitter disappointment." Indeed, these narratives highlight that genuine fulfillment surpasses material wealth. The pregnant waitress's fulfillment didn't stem from the unexpected money but from the realization that kindness and generosity could brighten even the darkest days.

Rod Stryker's Wisdom: Fulfilling One's Soul Purpose

Rod Stryker's wisdom underscores that long-term happiness and fulfillment are intimately tied to fulfilling one's soul's unique purpose. While Bryan Anderson and the anonymous lady in the cafe may not have known each other's names, they were united by a shared purpose—to extend help and inspire a chain of love. In doing so, they found a profound sense of fulfillment that transcended personal desires.

These stories exemplify that fulfillment is not a finite resource but a boundless wellspring. As individuals like Bryan Anderson and the kind-hearted lady pay forward the love and kindness they receive, the ripples of their actions extend far beyond themselves. The world is transformed one act of selfless service at a time, creating a tapestry of fulfillment that weaves together the collective good of humanity.

The Power of Fulfillment Through Service

The stories of Bryan Anderson, the pregnant waitress, and the anonymous lady in the cafe serve as profound reminders that fulfillment is not an elusive goal but a choice we make in each moment. True fulfillment is found not in the pursuit of personal desires but in the selfless act of helping others. It is in this act that we connect with our soul's purpose, echoing the wisdom of those who have walked this path before us. As we embrace the chain of love and kindness, we discover that fulfillment is not an end but a journey—a journey that beckons us to make a difference in the lives of others and, in turn, finds us fulfilled beyond measure.

Chapter 9:

The Ripple Effect of Change

The Ripple Effect of Change: Small Actions, Big Impacts

In the grand tapestry of life, it's often the smallest threads that create the most intricate patterns. This truth resonates strongly when we consider the ripple effect of change—the idea that small actions can lead to broader positive impacts in the world. Just as a pebble creates concentric ripples when dropped into a still pond, our individual efforts, no matter how modest, have the potential to shape the world around us in profound ways. Let's dive into the profound concept of the ripple effect and explore how even the tiniest acts of kindness, compassion, and change can catalyze transformation on a global scale.

The Butterfly Effect: A Whisper That Roars

The concept of the ripple effect is often likened to the "butterfly effect," a term coined in chaos theory. It suggests that the flapping of a butterfly's wings in one part of the world could set off a chain of events leading to a hurricane in another. While this analogy might seem far-fetched, it encapsulates the idea that small actions, when magnified and multiplied, can yield significant consequences. The seemingly insignificant acts of individuals can accumulate and gain momentum, sparking waves of change.

Acts of Kindness: A Smile That Brightens Lives

One of the simplest and most powerful ways the ripple effect manifests is through acts of kindness. A smile offered to a stranger can brighten their day, leading them to pass on that kindness to others they encounter. In this way, a single act of goodwill can create a cascade of positivity, fostering a more compassionate and interconnected society.

Compassion in Action: A Helping Hand That Heals Communities

Compassion is another force multiplier in the ripple effect of change. When individuals extend a helping hand to those in need, the impact transcends the immediate beneficiaries. Communities are strengthened, and a culture of empathy and support emerges. Acts of compassion resonate deeply, inspiring others to join the movement and make a collective difference.

Educational Initiatives: The Gift of Knowledge That Transforms Generations

Investments in education, no matter how localized, can lead to transformational change. When individuals teach, mentor, or support the education of others, they unlock the potential for exponential growth. Students who receive the gift of knowledge can go on to become educators themselves, passing on their wisdom to future generations.

Environmental Consciousness: Sustainable Choices That Impact the Planet

In an era when environmental concerns weigh heavily on our collective conscience, small individual actions can have a profound impact on the planet. Recycling, conserving energy, reducing waste, and making sustainable choices are examples of how everyday decisions can contribute to a healthier environment. When multiplied across communities, regions, and nations, these actions play a vital role in preserving our planet for future generations.

Innovation and Technology: Seeds of Progress That Revolutionize Society

Innovation often starts as a spark in the minds of a few visionary individuals. Yet, these small sparks have the potential to ignite fires of progress. Think of the inventors, scientists, and entrepreneurs whose pioneering work has transformed industries and societies. From Thomas Edison's lightbulb to the creators of life-saving vaccines, small innovations can reshape the world.

Leadership by Example: Inspiring Others to Follow Suit

Leaders who lead by example have an exceptional capacity to influence change. When leaders demonstrate integrity, resilience, and a commitment to positive values, they inspire those around them. Their actions set a standard that others aspire to emulate, creating a culture of excellence and ethical conduct.

Our Individual Power to Create Waves of Change

The ripple effect of change is a potent reminder of our individual power to shape the world. It emphasizes that no act of kindness, no matter how small, is insignificant. Whether through acts of compassion, educational initiatives, environmental stewardship, innovation, or leadership, our contributions have the potential to create waves of transformation that extend far beyond our immediate circles. The beauty of the ripple effect is that it calls us to action, encouraging us to be conscious of the impact we can make and the legacy we leave behind. As we embrace the profound interconnectedness of our actions, we realize that each one of us possesses the capacity to initiate positive change and create a brighter, more harmonious world for all.

Ignite Change with Questions: How Can You Assist and Uplift Others?

In the quest to make a positive impact on the lives of those around us, asking the right questions can be the spark that ignites transformation. Instead of waiting for opportunities to help and uplift, consider taking a proactive approach by asking yourself these empowering questions.

1. "Who Can I Assist Today?" Begin your day with this question, and let it guide your interactions. Whether it's a coworker, a neighbor, or a stranger, ponder who might benefit from your assistance.

2. "What Skills or Talents Can I Share?" Reflect on your unique talents and skills. How can you use them to benefit others? Whether it's teaching a skill, offering advice, or providing a service, your abilities can be a source of great support.

3. "How Can I Listen More Actively?" Effective listening is a powerful form of assistance. Ask yourself how you can improve your listening skills and be more present for those who need someone to talk to.

4. "Where Can I Volunteer or Donate?" Explore local organizations or causes that align with your values. Consider how you can contribute your time, resources, or expertise to support their mission.

5. "Whose Dreams Can I Encourage?" Think about the people in your life who have aspirations. How can you be a source of encouragement and motivation to help them pursue their dreams?

6. "What Acts of Kindness Can I Perform Randomly?" Random acts of kindness can brighten anyone's day. Challenge yourself to perform one unexpected act of kindness each day.

7. "How Can I Promote Inclusivity?" In a diverse world, inclusivity is crucial. Ask yourself how you can foster a more inclusive environment and advocate for those who may feel marginalized.

8. "What Can I Learn from Others?" Approach every interaction as an opportunity to learn. Ask questions, seek understanding, and grow from the wisdom of those you encounter.

9. "Am I Leading by Example?" Examine your own behavior and actions. Are you setting a positive example for those around you? How can you lead with integrity and compassion?

10. "How Can I Use My Network for Good?" Leverage your social network to create positive change. Connect people, share opportunities, and use your influence to uplift others.

11. "What Acts of Gratitude Can I Express?" Show appreciation to those who have supported you. Gratitude is a powerful way to uplift others and strengthen relationships.

12. "What Legacy of Upliftment Can I Leave?" Consider the long-term impact you want to have on the world. How can you leave a lasting legacy of assistance, kindness, and upliftment?

As you engage with these questions, remember that every small act of assistance and upliftment contributes to a brighter, more compassionate world. By actively seeking opportunities to make a difference, you become a beacon of positive change. So, ask these questions, and let your answers guide you on a journey of meaningful impact and transformation.

Chapter 10

Your Journey Begins - Key Takeaways from "The Power of Daily Questions: Transforming Your World One Question at a Time"

In "The Power of Daily Questions," we embark on a transformative journey that underscores the profound impact of asking the right questions in our lives. This book serves as a guide to help readers unlock their potential, ignite positive change, and foster personal growth through the practice of daily questioning. Here are the key takeaways that empower readers to start their daily question practice and embark on a path of proactive self-improvement and positive change:

1. Proactive Self-Improvement Through Daily Questions:

- Asking the right questions each day is the key to self-improvement and personal growth.
- By directing our focus and intention through daily questions, we can harness the power of self-reflection and awareness to chart our path to success.

2. Clarity of Goals:

- Daily questioning helps clarify our goals and aspirations.

- It prompts us to define what we truly want and the steps needed to achieve those goals.

3. Problem Solving and Creativity:

- Daily questions stimulate problem-solving abilities and creative thinking.
- They encourage us to find innovative solutions when faced with challenges.

4. Learning and Growth:

- Questions are a gateway to continuous learning, driving curiosity and a thirst for knowledge.
- They prompt us to seek answers, acquire new skills, and expand our horizons.

5. Cultivating a Positive Mindset:

- Daily questions can frame our mindset in a positive light.
- Questions that encourage gratitude and a focus on making a positive impact can foster optimism and resilience.

6. Adaptability in a Changing World:

- In a rapidly changing world, adaptability is a crucial skill.
- Questions about adapting to new situations or challenges keep us flexible and open to change.

7. Increased Accountability:

- Self-reflection holds us accountable for our actions and choices.
- Questions like, "Am I living in alignment with my values?" empower us to take ownership of our lives.

8. Creating Opportunities Through Problem-Solving:

- Problems and obstacles trigger positive thinking and birth opportunities.

- The ability to solve problems attracts opportunities in various aspects of life.

9. Upliftment and Compassion:

- Uplifting others and fostering compassion are central to personal growth and societal progress.
- Acts of kindness and support create a ripple effect of positive change.

10. Contentment and Fulfillment: - True contentment comes from embracing what we have and finding fulfillment in helping others. - By practicing gratitude and assisting those around us, we discover a deeper sense of purpose and happiness.

11. Creating Positive Change: - Life is about creativity and change, and positive change begins with us. - We have the power to use our resources to create a positive impact in our environment and the world.

12. Inspiring Action and Transformation: - Our actions, no matter how small, can lead to broader positive impacts in the world. - Leading by example and spreading positivity are effective ways to inspire change.

13. Unleashing Potential: - Each individual possesses untapped potential waiting to be unlocked. - Daily questions help us realize our unique capabilities and contribute to the world.

14. Leadership and Personal Growth: - Leadership is not something done to people; it's cultivated through personal growth. - Developing leadership skills is integral to realizing one's potential.

15. Continuous Self-Exploration: - Self-discovery is an ongoing process. - Encouraging questions such as, "What more can I learn about myself?" fosters personal growth.

16. The Ripple Effect of Change: - Small actions can lead to broader positive impacts. - Acts of kindness, compassion, and support create a ripple effect that can transform societies and the world.

17. Tolerance and True Wealth: - Tolerance and patience are essential virtues that contribute to a rich and fulfilling life. - True wealth resides in the heart, not just in one's financial pocket.

18. Inspiring Action and Transformation: - We can all contribute to positive change by asking how we can assist and uplift those around us. - Our actions, driven by kindness and compassion, have the power to inspire transformation.

19. Cultivating an Opportunity Mindset: - An opportunity mindset is cultivated through proactive questioning and a commitment to self-improvement. - It empowers us to create the life we desire.

20. Embrace Your Unique Journey: - Your journey of personal growth and transformation is unique to you. - Embrace it with an open heart and a commitment to continuous self-improvement.

Additional Resources for Personal Development and Self-Improvement:

- "The Power of Now" by Eckhart Tolle
- "Mindset: The New Psychology of Success" by Carol S. Dweck
- "Atomic Habits" by James Clear
- "The 7 Habits of Highly Effective People" by Stephen R. Covey
- "Daring Greatly" by Brené Brown
- "Start with Why" by Simon Sinek
- "Grit: The Power of Passion and Perseverance" by Angela Duckworth
- "The Miracle Morning" by Hal Elrod

These key takeaways and additional resources serve as a foundation for readers to embark on their personal journey of transformation and self-improvement. By embracing the power of daily questions and proactive change, each individual has the capacity to create a life filled with purpose, fulfillment, and positive impact

Appendices

Creating daily question journaling worksheets can be a helpful tool for individuals seeking to incorporate this practice into their daily routine. Here are several templates you can use or customize for your personal daily question journal:

1. Simple Daily Question Journal Template:

- Date: _____
- Today's Question: _____
- Your Reflection/Answer: _____
- Action Steps (if applicable): _____
- Gratitude Moment: _____

2. Goal-Oriented Daily Question Journal Template:

- Date: _____
- Today's Question: "What is one step I can take today toward my goal of _____?"
- Your Reflection/Answer: _____
- Action Steps: _____
- Affirmation/Mantra: _____

3. Problem-Solving Daily Question Journal Template:

- Date: _____
- Today's Challenge: _____
- Today's Question: "How can I overcome this challenge?"
- Your Reflection/Answer: _____
- Creative Solutions: _____

4. Gratitude and Positive Mindset Daily Question Journal Template:

- Date: _____
- Today's Question: "What am I grateful for today?"
- Your Reflection/Answer: _____
- Positive Affirmations: _____
- Acts of Kindness: _____

5. Self-Reflection and Personal Growth Daily Question Journal Template:

- Date: _____
- Today's Question: "What did I learn about myself today?"
- Your Reflection/Answer: _____
- Areas for Improvement: _____
- Goals for Tomorrow: _____

6. Creativity and Innovation Daily Question Journal Template:

- Date: _____
- Today's Question: "How can I approach my work/project/task differently today?"
- Your Reflection/Answer: _____
- Creative Ideas: _____
- Experimentation Plan: _____

7. Relationship and Connection Daily Question Journal Template:

- Date: _____
- Today's Question: "How can I deepen my connection with [person's name] today?"
- Your Reflection/Answer: _____
- Acts of Kindness: _____
- Quality Time Plans: _____

8. Mindfulness and Well-being Daily Question Journal Template:

- Date: _____
- Today's Question: "How can I practice self-care and mindfulness today?"
- Your Reflection/Answer: _____
- Mindfulness Practices: _____
- Gratitude Journal: _____

9. Leadership and Personal Growth Daily Question Journal Template:

- Date: _____
- Today's Question: "What leadership qualities can I cultivate today?"
- Your Reflection/Answer: _____
- Leadership Actions: _____
- Lessons Learned: _____

10. Weekly Reflection and Goal Setting Template:

- Date: _____
- Weekly Goal: _____
- Daily Questions:
- Monday: _____
- Tuesday: _____
- Wednesday: _____
- Thursday: _____
- Friday: _____
- Weekly Reflection: _____

Feel free to print or create digital versions of these templates for your daily question journaling practice. Adjust the questions and sections to align with your specific goals and needs. Consistency is key, so make it a habit to fill out your journal every day or at a frequency that works for you.

Offer recommended reading lists for further exploration of related topics.

Below, you'll find lists of recommended readings for further exploration of topics that align with those discussed in "The Power of Daily Questions: Transforming Your World One Question at a Time.:

Personal Growth and Self-Improvement:

- "The Power of Now: A Guide to Spiritual Enlightenment" by Eckhart Tolle
- "Mindset: The New Psychology of Success" by Carol S. Dweck
- "Atomic Habits: An Easy & Proven Way to Build Good Habits & Break Bad Ones" by James Clear
- "The 7 Habits of Highly Effective People" by Stephen R. Covey
- "Daring Greatly: How the Courage to Be Vulnerable Transforms the Way We Live, Love, Parent, and Lead" by Brené Brown

Problem Solving and Creativity:

- "Thinking, Fast and Slow" by Daniel Kahneman
- "Creativity, Inc.: Overcoming the Unseen Forces That Stand in the Way of True Inspiration" by Ed Catmull and Amy Wallace
- "Design Thinking: Understanding How Designers Think and Work" by Nigel Cross
- "Innovation and Entrepreneurship: Practice and Principles" by Peter F. Drucker
- "The Lean Startup: How Today's Entrepreneurs Use Continuous Innovation to Create Radically Successful Businesses" by Eric Ries

Mindfulness and Well-being:

- "Wherever You Go, There You Are: Mindfulness Meditation in Everyday Life" by Jon Kabat-Zinn
- "The Miracle of Mindfulness: An Introduction to the Practice of Meditation" by Thich Nhat Hanh
- "Radical Acceptance: Embracing Your Life With the Heart of a Buddha" by Tara Brach
- "The Body Keeps the Score: Brain, Mind, and Body in the Healing of Trauma" by Bessel van der Kolk
- "The Untethered Soul: The Journey Beyond Yourself" by Michael A. Singer

Leadership and Personal Development:

- "Start with Why: How Great Leaders Inspire Everyone to Take Action" by Simon Sinek
- "Leaders Eat Last: Why Some Teams Pull Together and Others Don't" by Simon Sinek
- "Grit: The Power of Passion and Perseverance" by Angela Duckworth
- "Leadership in War" by Andrew Roberts
- "Leadership and Self-Deception: Getting Out of the Box" by The Arbinger Institute

Gratitude and Positive Mindset:

- "The Gratitude Diaries: How a Year Looking on the Bright Side Can Transform Your Life" by Janice Kaplan
- "Thanks! How the New Science of Gratitude Can Make You Happier" by Robert A. Emmons
- "The Book of Joy: Lasting Happiness in a Changing World" by Dalai Lama, Desmond Tutu, and Douglas Carlton Abrams
- "The Power of Positive Thinking" by Norman Vincent Peale
- "The Happiness Advantage: The Seven Principles of Positive Psychology That Fuel Success and Performance at Work" by Shawn Achor

These reading lists offer a diverse range of books to explore and deepen your understanding of the concepts discussed in "The Power of Daily Questions." Whether you're interested in personal growth, problem-solving, mindfulness, leadership, or gratitude, these books provide valuable insights and guidance for your journey toward positive change and self-improvement.

Acknowledgments:

I would like to express my heartfelt gratitude to all those who contributed to the creation of this book, "The Power of Daily Questions: Transforming Your World One Question at a Time." Writing this book has been a labor of love and a journey of self-discovery, and I couldn't have done it without the support and inspiration of many individuals.

First and foremost, I want to thank my family and friends for their unwavering encouragement and belief in this project. Your constant support and patience during the writing process have been invaluable.

I am deeply thankful to my editor and the publishing team who saw the potential in this book and worked tirelessly to bring it to life. Your expertise and dedication have made this book a reality.

To the countless authors, thinkers, and researchers whose work has influenced the ideas presented in this book, thank you for sharing your wisdom with the world. Your insights have been a source of inspiration.

I also want to extend my gratitude to the readers who embark on this journey with me. Your curiosity and openness to exploring the power of daily questions are what make this endeavor worthwhile.

Lastly, to the universe or higher power that guides us all, thank you for the opportunities and challenges that have shaped my understanding of the world.

May this book serve as a source of inspiration and transformation for all who read it.

With profound gratitude,

Columbus Njikem

Author's Note:

Dear Reader,

It is with great pleasure and a sense of purpose that I present to you "The Power of Daily Questions." This book has been a labor of love, born out of a deep belief in the transformative potential of asking the right questions and the immense power that resides within each of us.

In these pages, you will embark on a journey of self-discovery, personal growth, and positive change. The concept of daily questions is not just a theoretical idea; it is a practical tool that can be applied to your everyday life. It has the potential to ignite your curiosity, unlock your potential, and lead you toward a more fulfilling and purpose-driven existence.

As you read, I encourage you to engage actively with the content. Take the time to ponder the questions posed, reflect on your own experiences, and consider how you can apply these principles to your unique journey. Remember that the true value of this book lies in the actions you take as a result of the insights gained.

I also want to emphasize that you are not alone on this journey. Countless individuals around the world are seeking personal growth and positive change, just like you. By embracing the power of daily questions, you join a global community of seekers and change-makers who are committed to making a difference, starting with themselves.

I invite you to keep an open heart and mind as you explore the chapters that follow. Embrace the challenges, celebrate the victories, and, most importantly, take proactive steps toward the positive change you desire.

Thank you for choosing to embark on this journey with me. May the insights and practices you discover within these pages inspire you to transform your world, one question at a time.

With gratitude and optimism,

Columbus Njikem

In "The Power of Daily Questions: Transforming Your World One Question at a Time," we have explored a range of concepts related to personal growth, problem-solving, mindfulness, leadership, gratitude, and creating positive change. To deepen your understanding and continue your journey toward personal transformation, consider exploring the following references and recommended reading:

1. "The Power of Now: A Guide to Spiritual Enlightenment" by Eckhart Tolle: This book delves into the concept of mindfulness and living in the present moment, which is a foundational aspect of daily question practice.

2. "Atomic Habits: An Easy & Proven Way to Build Good Habits & Break Bad Ones" by James Clear: Explore the science of habit formation and how small daily changes can lead to significant personal growth.

3. "Start with Why: How Great Leaders Inspire Everyone to Take Action" by Simon Sinek: Understand the importance of purpose and motivation in leadership and personal development.

4. "The Gratitude Diaries: How a Year Looking on the Bright Side Can Transform Your Life" by Janice Kaplan: Learn about the transformative power of gratitude and how it can reshape your mindset and daily practices.

5. "Thinking, Fast and Slow" by Daniel Kahneman: Delve into the psychology of decision-making and understand how to make more informed choices in your daily life.

6. "The Miracle of Mindfulness: An Introduction to the Practice of Meditation" by Thich Nhat Hanh: Discover mindfulness techniques and meditation practices that can enhance your daily question rituals.

7. "Leaders Eat Last: Why Some Teams Pull Together and Others Don't" by Simon Sinek: Explore the concept of leadership that prioritizes the well-being of the team and fosters a positive work environment.

8. "Design Thinking: Understanding How Designers Think and Work" by Nigel Cross: Gain insights into problem-solving methodologies and the creative process, which can inform your daily questioning practices.

9. "The Lean Startup: How Today's Entrepreneurs Use Continuous Innovation to Create Radically Successful Businesses" by Eric Ries: Learn about the principles of lean thinking and innovation, which can be applied to personal growth and problem-solving.

10. "The Untethered Soul: The Journey Beyond Yourself" by Michael A. Singer: Explore the concept of inner freedom and the transformational power of self-awareness and self-inquiry.

These recommended readings offer diverse perspectives and practical tools for self-improvement, personal growth, and positive change. Whether you are interested in developing mindfulness, enhancing your leadership skills, or fostering gratitude in your life, these books provide valuable insights and guidance. As you continue your journey of self-discovery and transformation, these references can serve as valuable companions and sources of inspiration.

Made in the USA
Middletown, DE
19 November 2023